Using real-life situations, conflicts, and solutions,
this book will help you:

—— Understand your parents' problems—and how
they affect you

—— Learn why parents sometimes feel the need
to be right

—— Deal with nagging, grouchiness, criticism,
overprotectiveness, and parents'
embarrassing behavior, in new and better
ways

—— Communicate with your parents about sex,
drugs, and other hot topics

—— Accept that sometimes life simply isn't fair

—— Come to terms with your feelings about your
parents as people

—— Cope with a stepparent
...and more

By Joyce L. Vedral, Ph.D.
Published by Ballantine Books:

I DARE YOU—HOW TO GET WHAT YOU
WANT OUT OF LIFE

MY PARENTS ARE DRIVING ME CRAZY

I CAN'T TAKE IT ANY MORE

JOYCE L. VEDRAL, Ph.D.

MY PARENTS ARE DRIVING ME CRAZY

BALLANTINE BOOKS • NEW YORK

Library of Congress Catalog Card Number: 86-90929
ISBN 0-345-33011-0

Manufactured in the United States of America

First Edition: October 1986
Fifth Printing: May 1988

This book is dedicated to my parents—Martha and David Yellin, because if they didn't drive me crazy, I would never have been able to write this book, and to every teenager whose parents are driving them crazy—including my own daughter, Marthe Simone Vedral. (If she would read this book, I would stop driving her crazy.)

– TABLE OF CONTENTS –

– ACKNOWLEDGMENTS –

Thank you Barbara and Joe Vale for your hilarious stories.

Thank you to every parent who volunteered to be interviewed for this book.

Thank you Marthe Simone Vedral, Jennifer Berkowitz, Allison Limmer, Rob D'Avanzo, Alex That, Brian Loughlin, and Dave Leahy, Kim Elman, Jason Vale, Jared Vale and the students of Julia Richman High School for reading parts of this book, and for contributing your real-life experiences.

Thank you Marilyn Abraham for your brilliant editing.

Thank you Liz Williams for your continual enthusiasm.

– INTRODUCTION –

Look, I don't know what to say or where to start so I'll just plunge in right here. This book is great! It's not like some corny self-help book where you read one page and throw it! This is reality! We're talking about problems you would have with your parents in the 80's, not on *Little House on the Prairie*. If you have trouble dealing with your parents this book has helpful advice on every difficult situation.

My mother wrote this book so you're probaby saying, "Yeah, she's full of it." But this really can get you out of trouble, sticky situations, etc. Me and all my friends read it and use it successfully.

Now don't get me wrong. This book is not a guaranteed cure for all fighting with your parents, but it can make life with them a lot easier. I'm not saying I never fight with my mother anymore. It's just that I know exactly how to stop the fight and turn things around. We were in the car one day and I was arguing with her for not letting me go out and do anything with my friends. She's so overprotective. I remembered an idea in the book and said, "Mommy, just for one minute, remember back to when you were fourteen. Can you picture it?" She did. Then I said, "Mommy, how would you feel if your mother didn't let you go anywhere or do anything?" She said, "I see your point. I'll think about this matter." The next week she let me do something that I had been begging her about for a long time.

This book helped me to understand my mother, and to realize that when your mother or father does something embarrassing it is no big deal. Also, it shows why parents might be grouchy and tells you how to change their mood all the way around with just a comment or a kind word. It explains that your parents are having a hard time letting you be free and independent because they know the dangers in the world and are afraid you might meet up with them. If you have a long talk with your parents explaining that you understand the dangers that are out there, your parents might feel you're more responsible than they thought you were.

You'll have to read the book for yourself because chances are, everyone isn't running to help you with your problems. You've got to help yourself, so read the book and take the advice. I know, because I've experienced it and used it.

—*Marthe Simone Vedral, 14*

1

My Parents Are Driving Me Crazy— Why Are They Doing This to Me?!

Parents can be a problem. They can make your life so miserable that you think you just can't take it anymore. Sometimes you wish you could make them over—take away some of the most annoying traits they have and add in some of the qualities you want. What would your perfect parents be like? Allison, 15, says,

> If I could create perfect parents, they wouldn't nag so much and they would trust me and believe in me instead of always looking at the negative side. They would give me credit for things and be loving and understanding. I'd be able to tell them anything and not have to worry about the consequences.

It would be nice if we could change people just like that. We'd probably have more friends, and get along more easily with everyone. The trouble is no one person can change another ... unless that person *wants* to change. And therein lies the trick.

Although you may not be able to change your parents, you *can* do something to change the way your parents treat you. You *can* help them want to change. In order to do this, however, you have to learn a little about adults and the way they think. If you can understand the psychological reasons for their behavior, you will be better able to *get* and *give* what is needed in your relationship with them.

There are thousands of books on the market for parents on how to cope with, understand, and put up with their teenagers' behavior but no real books for teenagers on how to cope with parental behavior. This is a first.

It's kind of daring for a teenager to take the initiative to improve the relationship with his or her parents. Usually it's the other way around. The trouble with that method, however, is it's too one-sided. Thus it never really works. In order to effect changes in the way things are going at home you, too, will have to do some of the understanding, analyzing, and talking. To begin with, you will have to understand the way your parent is thinking. It isn't as difficult as you may think.

By the time you finish applying the ideas in this book, your parents will be more loving, understanding, cooperative, and whatever else is missing in them now. As a bonus, you will forgive your parents for not being perfect and you will have compassion or mercy for them.

Since your parents have already been teenagers, they know at least something about being teenagers, even if they didn't read any books about it and *seem* to have forgotten everything about their own experiences. You, on the other hand, were never an adult and so know relatively little about what it feels like to be, say, forty years old.

Well, it is critical that you find out, and this book will give you that chance. It will help you to understand why your parents sometimes make your life miserable by nagging, screaming, punishing, being too strict, embarrassing you, treating you like a baby, acting grouchy, and criticizing everything you do. It will even help you to handle that stepparent you hate, so that he or she is no longer the bane (deadly poison) of your life.

A bad relationship with your parents can paralyze you for life. It can make you believe, unconsciously, that you are not a good person. You may suppress a continual guilt, blaming yourself for the bad relationship. You may suffer from a low self-esteem and may expect to fail no matter what the goal. You may become a self-made loser.

If things get bad enough, escaping through lots of alcohol and drugs may seem an attractive idea. If that doesn't do it, you may try to find the missing love in sexual encounters. Finally, you may get so depressed and frustrated you may even think of suicide.

But there's no need for any of these things to happen. You have a will. You can use the power of the will that resides in you to change what is happening in your life. "If you lacked the strength and only had the will, I could have helped you," said Goethe, a famous writer. Well, I'm telling you now: If you have the will—if you want to succeed, if you want to make things better, I can help you. No matter how weak you are, no matter how depressed you are, no matter how bad things are, I can help you—to help yourself.

– THE THREE MOST BASIC REASONS YOUR PARENTS DRIVE YOU CRAZY –

1. *No one ever went to school to learn how to be a parent.* Even if there were special schools that gave courses in every aspect of parenting, the graduates would still have to wait until they had real children of their own to know

how to parent. You see, when it comes to being a parent, there's no way to learn except by doing. Because of this fact, parents naturally make a lot of mistakes. It isn't easy for them—so many decisions all the time. They really want what's best for you, but they don't always make the right choices. What would you do if you had to make all the decisions and accept all the responsibilities in your home for just one week or even for just a day? How about on a job in which there is no one there to train you? Wouldn't you make some mistakes?

2. *Your parent is getting older*. Not old. Just older. Stop for a moment and picture yourself at forty. See what you look like. Imagine what your goal will be. What will be on your mind. Stop and really get a picture of it. I asked some teenagers this question. Simone, 14, said,

> My life is basically over. I have nothing to get excited about. I look forward to baby-sitting for my grand-children some day and then dying.

Dawn, 15, said,

> Forget about it. I'm out of shape and over the hill. I've had my fun already. I go to work, come home, make dinner, watch TV, and go to sleep. Who cares?

Paul, 16, said,

> I can't picture being that old. It's impossible. I'll always be young.

But you will get that old. If you're lucky. And when you do, you may think that life begins at forty. Simone and Dawn and Paul will want to have fun and live. Most of your parents are facing a second chance at life now. Let me explain why.

Up until now your parents have been living hard and

fast. They've passed from being babies to children to teens to adults, but all the time they never really thought that someday it would end. They were so busy living that they didn't have time to say, "What's it all about. When am I really going to start enjoying life?"

As a person comes close to forty, that person seemingly approaches the top of a mountain. It is as if he or she were climbing for forty years and could not see what was on the other side of the mountain. Reaching forty—the top of the mountain—is a shock. Suddenly you realize that life does end some day. It is as if you look down the mountain to the bottom and you clearly see the valley. At first you get scared. "I will die someday," you say. But then you get excited. Very excited. You say, "I have only about forty years left. What will I do with the rest of my time? I'd better make some quick moves. It's time to reevaluate priorities."

But right in the middle of this new realization, there *you* are. You are a teenager with a world of troubles of your own. And what's worse, you expect your parents to help you out with those troubles. But sometimes your parent wants to be free to pursue his or her life. The problem is your parents can't just flit off and take a trip around the world or quit their jobs and become forest rangers at a low salary. They have responsibilities. They must *Keep Going*, like it or not. And at times, many times, whether they tell you about it or not, they don't like it.

Don't misunderstand, and please don't be angry. It isn't as if they don't like you. It's not that they wish to abandon you. That would be the last thing they would want to do. They consider you to be one of the best things that happened to them in their entire lives, and most parents tell me they wish they had had even more children. But the cold, hard fact of life is, your parents are facing a tough time in their lives and they do need some time to explore life. Denied this, they will become grouchy and irritable. They may do all sorts of things that can be a problem to you. When this happens, you can either make things worse by becoming demanding and attacking and criticizing them, or you can make things better by understanding them and sympathizing with them.

3. *Your parents say hurtful things when they feel frustrated or misunderstood.* "Hey, wait a minute!" you might say. "I'm the one who needs understanding!" Well, I agree. You do need it. But so do your parents. And if you give it, you will get it. This may be a whole new idea. But it's also a fact.

Did your parent ever say,

I can't wait until you're out of this house,

or   If I knew what it would be like, I would never have had children,

or   just wait until *you* have children.

Now that you know just a little about parents, you can perhaps understand such comments. Some teenagers have reported to me that in the heat of anger their parents have even said, "I curse the day you were born," or "I hate you." All the parents were really saying is "I'm frustrated. I can't cope with the responsibility of dealing with you. My own life is slipping away. I'm scared."

Instead of hating your parents because they sometimes hurt you, why not take the situation in hand. I challenge you to refuse to accept the status quo. I dare you to use your head to change your life. You don't have to be a genius to use the ideas in this book. You need only the will. Remember: "If you lacked the strength and only had the will, I could have helped you."

I believe you have the will. If you didn't, you would have put this book down after reading page one.

2

Your Parents' Ten Basic Problems

There are ten basic problems facing your parents. If you take the time to analyze and understand these problems, you may be able to change what happens at home. Instead of unwittingly plunging into arguments with your parents, you may find yourself skilled at avoiding fights. You could stop them dead when they are nagging and you could change their grouchy moods into happy ones. You might even hear them add kind words to their criticism of you!

It's important to understand your parents' problems as best as you can. If you ignore their troubles, your own will undoubtedly increase.

Consider the list below:

1. Your parents are physically tired. They are not sixteen anymore.

2. Your parents are going into middle age, while you are

going into your prime. They often miss the child that used to look up to them.

3. Your parents want to have fun. They are nervous about growing old. Seeing you grow up makes them feel older.

4. Your parents know they have made some mistakes. They want to protect you from making these mistakes.

5. Your parents have pressures: job, money, relationships, other family members, unfulfilled goals, etc.

6. Your parents are living in a different world from what existed when they were teenagers. They sometimes see it as dangnerous.

7. Your parents had their own set of parents, who made mistakes with them. They may be insecure, neurotic, etc.

8. Your parents have certain values (beliefs) that they want to pass on to you, and that they are afraid you won't accept.

9. Your parents have wisdom. They have lived a long time. They want to save you from the pitfalls of life, yet they also must accept that wisdom cannot be given. You have to find your way to it on your own.

10. Your parents secretly feel guilty and anxious for not being perfect parents.

These ten problems are at the roots of your parents' seemingly impossible behavior, so you might as well take a closer look at what's going on for them. Of course, later on we will focus on how you can turn your parents' words and deeds around. But for now it is important that you realize the most significant tool you have in forging a good relationship with your parents is *Your* understanding. The rest will come.

1. *Your parents are physically tired. They are not sixteen anymore.*

Even though your parents have less energy than you do, very often they do more work than you do. They get up early and go off to work. Then they come home and have to deal with the household chores and other family members. Because they are physically tired, they may become annoyed when they see anything that represents work, like a messy house.

Sometimes your parents will make unjust demands just because they are exhausted. You may be summoned to go to the store immediately for something your mother forgot to pick up on the way home from work. She is tired, and she believes that you have more energy than she does. Also, you can be sure that you will be nagged if you were supposed to do a chore and it is still undone when your mother or father comes home from work tired. They think that you are out having fun all day while they are exhausting themselves working hard for you and the family.

2. *Your parents are going into middle age, while you are going into your prime. They often miss the child that used to look up to them.*

Sometimes your parents get depressed when they see you growing up. It reminds them that they are getting older. You are going into the most energetic, exciting time of your life, while they are approaching eventual old age. One mother says,

I was walking with my daughter and someone whistled. I turned around and my daughter said, "Not you, Ma." I said, "How do you know? People still whistle at me." But then I thought, She's probably right. Who am I kidding?

If you play the music too loud when your father comes home from work and he just happens to be depressed because someone called him Pop at work, he may demand that you turn the music off immediately. If you ask your mother to drive you to the shopping mall after she just discovered she gained five pounds and thought to herself, "middle-aged spread," don't be surprised if she lectures you that "Life does not revolve around you." In effect, sometimes your parents look at you and it is as if you are a mirror reflecting the fact that they are getting older. Don't forget, when you were a child, you admired them and looked up to them. You didn't argue with them much, and you weren't critical. You ever told your mother that her hairstyle was out, and you never picked on your father for wearing too much jewelry, etc. Teenagers help their parents to see that they are not young, and this sometimes causes irritability and grouchiness.

3. *Your parents want to have fun. They are nervous about growing old. One father says,*

I'm on their level. They don't want me to be on their level. They want me to be an old fart.

Does your parent ever embarrass you? Do your parents seem to forget what they're supposed to be (in your eyes) and behave in foolish way sometimes? One mother says,

I was on the beach and a good song came on the radio. I started snapping my fingers and dancing around. Karen got so embarrassed she walked away from me. I couldn't figure it out. What am I supposed to do, get in a box and die?

This mother couldn't understand why her thirteen-year-old daughter was so embarrassed. I know and you know it is because teenagers like parents to keep their place. It's unsettling when parents try to dress or behave in a manner that demonstrates the uninhibitedness of youth. But parents get tired of playing the role of parent or adult. They want to have fun, too.

4. *Your parents know they have made some mistakes. They want to protect you from making these mistakes.*

You may wonder why you seem to be getting the same lecture over and over again. For example, you may hear the one about "don't get too serious with anyone, you're too young. There's plenty of time." Maybe your mother is like this thirty-seven-year-old mother:

> I had to get married. It was because I had a steady boyfriend at a very young age. I was pregnant at sixteen. Now I have three children, and two of them are teenagers. I feel like I'm fifty instead of thirty-seven. I lost my youth.

This father's favorite theme is college:

> I always tell my son, "Schooling is everything. Go to school." I should have become a lawyer, but no, I had to go and quit. Now I have to work hard for every dollar. My son is going to be a professional. I'll see to that.

Because of your parents' mistakes, you hear many lectures on how to avoid the same pitfalls. After a while, you may become tired of hearing them. Still, be kind, and listen to your parents even if it bores you. Your not listening only makes them repeat the lecture more often. They may even say something helpful. Remember, their intentions are good. They want to save you from what they see as a bad life. The trouble is, they often don't know when they are fighting imaginary enemies. You may have no intention of making the mistake they fear. It is up to you to help them see this. Later, you will find out how.

5. *Your parents have pressures: job, money, relationships, other family members, unfulfilled goals, etc.*

Although your parents want to have fun and be free, they often cannot, because of responsibilities. This causes pressure and tension. They may become grouchy and irritable and they may nag you.

If the roof develops a leak or the car stalls, it's up to them to fix it. If one of the other children becomes very sick, they have to care for that person. You can blissfully ignore these problems, but your parent has to deal with them. Your mother may have to give up her night at the gym or your father his card game to deal with home responsibilites. These are outlets your parents look forward to.

In addition, parents, believe it or not, still have a love life—or lack of one. Whether it's a rough time in their marriage, or your single parent's dating life, they can become upset by problems of the heart.

I always know when my mother has a fight with her boyfriend. All you have to do is ask her a simple question and she jumps down your throat. We all know when to stay away.

This fifteen-year-old has figured out when to avoid her mother and she does.

At times they will become angry bcause it seems as if the pressure is too much and there's no escaping it. They think, "Why can't someone else take care of it." But there *is* no someone else. They're *it*.

6. *Your parents are living in a different world from what existed when they were teenagers. They sometimes see it as dangerous.*

Think about this: When your parents were teenagers television was new, computers were the size of football fields, and there were no skateboards, no Walkmen, and no video games. Abortions were illegal, the pill didn't exist, and only hard-core drug addicts did drugs. College was a luxury, not a necessity. People didn't always lock their doors, and violent crime was the exception rather than the rule.

Because the world has changed so much, your parents often fear you are not safe in it. They try to protect you and may seem to baby you or behave in an old-fashioned manner. They may nag you to be prepared for the technology, and they may lecture you to be careful about crime in the streets. They worry constantly that you will succumb to the available drugs, and they may act as if they suspect you of doing drugs. All of this behavior stems from their fear that they won't be able to keep you safe in the expanding, changing world. Their intentions are good. They love you. And if you think about what the world was like when they were your age, (See the film *Back to the Future* to get an idea) you can surely understand why they sometimes get nervous.

7. *Your parents had their own set of parents, who made mistakes with them. As a result, they may be insecure, neurotic, angry, nervous, etc.*

Your grandparents, all four of them, were as troublesome to your parents as your parents are to you. At times your grandparents treated your parents unfairly. They nagged and criticized your parents and may on many occasions have caused them to feel insecure about themselves. They may even have exacted old-fashioned discipline that today would be labeled child abuse. Your parents learned some of their best and worst "parenting" habits from their parents.

Stop and think about it. Your parents and their parents and the parents before them all the way down the line were all influenced by parents, and none of these parents was perfect. It's little wonder your parents may seem to have psychological imbalances—spots of off behavior or some oddities. Probably, all things considered, your parents are doing the best they can with what they have to work with. I always tell my daughter, "I'm operating with a full deck, but the cards are tattered and some of them are chewed up a bit. But I'm doing the best I can."

We can't choose our parents. The same way you didn't choose yours, your parents didn't choose theirs, and the children you have will not have chosen you. Maybe if you ask your parents questions about their childhood and teenage years, it would help you to see why they behave the way they do. I think you will be surprised how your attitude toward them changes.

8. *Your parents have certain values (beliefs) that they want to pass on to you.*

Your values are what you believe is right and wrong—they are your philosophy of life. Your parents have ideas about right and wrong, some of them that they have absorbed from their own parents and some of them that they have figured out from living. Naturally your parents hope that you will share their values. For example, if your father believes that fairness is important, he will be disappointed if he sees you taking advantage of someone. If a mother believes that girls should not call boys, she will nag her daughter when she tries to telephone a boy.

Every time she calls a boy, I cringe. That's no way to do things. A boy likes to be the aggressor.

This mother may believe that she is right, but her daughter says,

She's living in the middle ages. Now girls call boys all the time. I don't see anything wrong with it.

Most parents have basic humanitarian values, and when they see you seemingly rejecting these values, they become upset. This father says,

I teach my boys to follow the Golden Rule and to keep the Ten Commandments. I tell them that if they do, they'll have no problems they can't handle. When Joey got caught cheating, I could have died. I was heartbroken.

It's the most natural thing in the world for your parents to want you to accept their values. Of course you won't want to accept all of them, as you will eventually develop your own set of values. But chances are one day you, too, will try to influence your own children to accept your values. Maybe you will remember to give them a little room, and maybe you won't . . . !

9. *Your parents have wisdom. They have lived a long time.*

Your parents have been around for a while, and they know things. They've seen the road and know the potholes. Their goal is to warn you about them so that you can save yourself unnecessary pain.

Parents may tell you to "Be careful, that's a dangerous sport," or "Don't drink. You need your wits about you," or "Don't hang out with that crowd. They could get you into trouble." At times they play a movie in their minds and imagine you falling into traps they know about. Then they desperately try to warn you, but you brush them off, saying, "I know, I know," all the time thinking that your parents are worrying for nothing. But they're not. They've been around and they *know* things can happen.

A good example is a case where a parent makes light of a deep love you have, a love that left you heartbroken. He or she may say, "Don't worry. There are plenty of fish in the sea." You think, "He doesn't understand," or "She doesn't know how I feel." But your parent does know that you can fall in deep love again, deeper and even more satisfying. Your parent does remember when his or her heart was broken and when he or she thought the world would end. The thing is, your parent later found out that a better love can come along.

If you listen to your parents when they try to teach you some truth, instead of ignoring them, they will lighten up a bit and not feel compelled to preach.

10. *Your parents fear that they are not being good parents. They often secretly feel guilty and anxious for not being perfect parents.*

Parents say things to themselves like

> I wonder if I'm doing the right thing by...
> It's probably my fault that Sandy...
> I could kick myself for...
> I knew I should have...

They continually blame themselves for your unhappiness, often seeking reasons for it in their own mistakes at parenting. Because they are trying so hard to do a good job, they often become frustrated when there are problems in your life. Instead of telling you that they blame themselves, however, they may suppress this expression and angrily blame you. But inside, all the time, they're thinking, "It's my fault."

When you get into serious trouble, their guilt makes them even more irritable. Their rage at you may well be rage at themselves for not having provided the right guidance for you. Of course, in reality, many of the things that go wrong are not their fault. One, they cannot be perfect parents, and two, you have your own mind. They should not blame themselves for everything you do wrong. Much is your decision. But they frequently do.

The ten basic problems described in this chapter hold the key to why your parents behave the way they do. Now you know what's making them tick.

Well, it's time to act!!!

Your parents don't expect things to change. They're going along under the assumption that life will continue the way it is. Use this to your advantage! Start using psychology with your parents and catch them off-guard. Your efforts will delight them, and they will find themselves being more loving and cooperative. All of you will find that life can be happier and less frustrating.

These ten problems will undoubtedly still haunt your parents ... but if you keep this book in mind, they won't haunt you!

3

Nag! Nag! Nag!

If they gave degrees for nagging, my father would be a black belt.

According to most teenagers, parents nag. Chances are, you would agree. They harp on everything from keeping your room neat to taking out the garbage, from using the bathroom to the way you dress, from your choice of friends to your marks and homework. There seems to be no end to what parents nag about.

Why do they nag? They nag because no one is listening, or at least no one is letting on that they are. The more they feel ignored, the more they nag.

Trying to pretend you don't hear them is similar to ignoring a slow leak in a tire. Sooner or later the tire will go flat, and you'll be forced to pay attention. Sooner or later your parent will *make you* take notice, by screaming, issuing an extreme punishment, or even worse.

I asked some teenagers why they don't listen when their parents talk to them or nag. Linda, 13, says,

I don't want to hear it. I just don't want to listen.

Jenny, 14, says,

You just can't take it. You know all about it already, so you look away....

But the more you tune them out, the more they nag. As much as it kills you, if you want to see changes around your house, you'll have to break your old habit of tuning them out.

Here is a three-step plan to stop your parents from nagging:

1. Listen to the nag and figure out why they are harping on that point.

2. Indicate that you understand their point.

3. Follow up by taking immediate action to remove the reason for their nag.

Learn to listen. Instead of tuning your parents out the minute they begin talking, stop and pay attention to what they're saying. Ask questions, too. It will prove your interest.

– "CLEAN UP NOW" NAGGING –

If your mother is going on and on about "the house is a mess," ask her what exactly hits her eye and makes her angry. She may then say, "The crumpled towels, the dishes in the sink, your messy room." You can then answer with something like, "I'm sorry. You're right. Things are a mess. I'll pick up the towels and then clean my room." Then start doing something immediately. If you have trouble being so flexible, just review the list of ten problems in the previous chapter. Your parent may have come home tired, frustrated, or angry. The messy house was the last straw. Can you really blame her?

Stephanie, 16, says,

> When my mother came home from work, she started nagging about the fact that I didn't clean the house or throw out the garbage yet. She said, "You can't do anything right around here, but when it comes to going out, you do that right." I said, "When it comes to nagging, you do that right." She started screaming at me and I walked away and closed the door to my room to shut out her voice. She burst in wildly, yelling that I was going to be punished. . . .

If Stephanie had analyzed why her mother was nagging, using the list, she might have come to a few intelligent conclusions. Her mother may be harping on something because she is tired. (1) She has just come home from a hard day's work. (2) There may be pressure at her job. (3) She may be feeling resentful that Stephanie is young and having all the fun, while she is getting older and has to do all the work.

Had Stephanie thought about it, she might have conducted herself differently. Perhaps the conversation would have gone as follows after her mother said, "You can't do anything right around here, but when it comes to going out, you do that right." Stephanie might say,

> It must make you sick to come home after working so hard to see the house this dirty. I can see why you think all I care about is having fun. But that's not always true. It's just that sometimes I forget about your problems and just think about my life.

I'm sorry. I'll take out the garbage right now and get started on my room.

Before you throw this book across the room and say, "That's idiotic. I'll never say that to my mother," think of the results the above conversation might have! Stephanie's mother would do a double take. She would immediately stop nagging and calm down. Next, she would be happy that Stephanie showed compassion for her problems. Then she would be delighted to see that Stephanie realizes at times she is self-centered. Finally, she would be appeased by Stephanie's willingness to do something about the situation right away.

Remember, the basic formula is

• Listen and analyze.
• Show understanding and compassion.
• Take immediate action.

What may seem like a ridiculous submission on your part will turn into a major victory. You will actually stop major nagging.

You may say as you read, but why should I be the nice one, and why should I do the thing I'm being nagged about. Well, anyone can do the easy thing, and argue back, attack the nagger verbally, defend him or herself. (Stephanie did both.) But think of this. Where will it get you? The answer is, more nagging, maybe some screaming, and quite possibly a punishment. Is yelling back worth it?

If you are serious about changing your parents' behavior, you're going to have to start taking some chances—start stepping out on a limb. You'll have to start saying things to your parents that demonstrate the attitude of a psychologist. In fact, you'll have to start thinking from your parents' mind, imagining where they are coming from, and you'll have to start reflecting back to your parents, in words, their own views and feelings.

– "HOW MANY TIMES
DO I HAVE TO TELL YOU"
NAGGING –

One of the things teenagers hate most about nagging is their abhorrence for being told more than once. Parents have an answer to this:

Do it and I won't nag. (mother)

Pick up the shoes, do the dishes, show respect, and I won't have to repeat myself. (father)

Listen to me the first time, and I won't have to say it again. (mother)

Parents are frustrated because they believe that you're not getting the message. Their proof is nothing gets done. And what is nagging, really, but repeating the same message over and over again. *Parents do not enjoy nagging!*

The only way to stop them from repeating that message over and over is to get the message. It's like knocking on a door. First you knock, then when no one answers, you knock louder. Still no answer? You bang on the door. Finally you kick the door. Especially if you know your friend is home. Maybe you just saw him go in through the door. You won't go away. You'll keep trying because you know that person is there.

When something is important to your parents, they will not give up until you hear them. They'll come at you from every angle. Yet many teenagers continue to ignore their parents when they nag.

I don't answer a word. I just get angry.

Charlie, *15*

I ignore it. That's my method. Even if I know she's right, I won't give her the satisfaction.

Joe, *14*

I'm used to it. I know he nags because he's worrying out loud about me. I just keep doing whatever I'm doing without answering him.

Donna, *17*

He knows my schedule. Why should I tell him why I didn't mow the lawn yet?

Dave, *16*

I just squinch my face and say, "Please, Mom, don't start."

Karen, *16*

It's insulting to ignore parents in these ways. No wonder they become furious! Most teenagers wouldn't treat friends or even acquaintances that way.

– "YOU KNOW I CAN'T STAND IT WHEN YOU DO THAT" NAGGING –

Some parents nag about seemingly unimportant things, but to the parent it *is* important. Such nagging can be the result of a simple difference in basic personalities. For example, William says,

She gets on my nerves. Always has to have everything perfect. For example, we usually keep our shoes on a mat when we come in. If one isn't straight, she'll right it with the other one. She nags us to death because everything has to be in tip-top condition. She reminds me of Felix Unger of *The Odd Couple*.

William makes the point beautifully. He and his mother are about as compatible as Felix and Oscar of the Odd Couple—two opposites, one a perfectionist, the other a lover of disorder. Since none of us chooses our parents, we all have to find ways to live with parents who are opposites. William has two choices. He can say something like

Mom, You are such a perfectionist. I can't stand it. You're always picking on stupid things.

Of course this would bring on a major fight and his mother would nag more than ever. Or, he can try to see things from his mother's point of view and say something like

Sometimes I wonder where I get my genes. You are a real perfectionist, and I am just the opposite! We remind me of *The Odd Couple*. I'll really try to be neater, but I think no matter what I DO, I'll still be an annoyance to you.

Such words will comfort Mrs. Perfectionist. She'll focus on the fact that her son is different and that she has a very high standard of neatness for her house. She may still nag, but the anger and fury will be largely reduced.

– "CAN'T YOU STAY HOME MORE" NAGGING –

Another typical reason for parental nagging is their longing for more attention. As you grow up, they notice that your life no longer includes them. You're always out with your friends. Eighteen-year-old Chris seems to be in this situation.

My father nags me about the stupidest things. He's always complaining, "The only reason you come home is to eat and sleep." Everytime he says that, I grit my teeth. It seems as if he's daring me to answer him in a smart way, but I just sit there and try to ignore him. Lots of times the things he says are correct. I know I should spend more time at home, but I don't think he should nag so much.

Chris admits he knows his father is often right but then confesses to ignoring it. Wouldn't it be easier for Chris to express this simple thought to his father:

Dad, you're right. I should spend more time at home. I have so many friends and my life is so busy, I feel as if I'm just checking in and out of here as if it were a hotel. (In saying this, Chris would be reflecting back his father's feelings, and this would comfort his father.) I miss spending time with you and the family, too. I'll have to plan my life a little more carefully.

Chris's father would be happy to see that Chris realizes it isn't right to totally ignore your family, and he would be secretly thrilled to hear that Chris misses spending time with the family (him). Instead of nagging, he would probably start talking about how he misses the days when Chris spent more time with him and the family. He might even admit to how hard it is to see his son grow up, knowing that he will eventually leave the nest. Chris could then comfort his father by saying he understands how difficult it must be, and that he certainly doesn't want to abandon anyone. He just wants to grow up.

Teenagers don't sympathize with and listen to their parents very often, so when one wise teen does, it really softens the heart of the adult. I know that when my daughter or one of the teenagers I teach sympathizes with me, it turns my bad mood around and makes my heart feel as light and merry as if I didn't have a care in the world. After that, I say to myself, "What was I so upset about?"

Teens, you just don't know how much power you have. Use it.

– "WHY MUST YOU LOOK LIKE THAT" NAGGING –

Finally, many parents have a habit of nagging about things related to your personal appearance. They constantly repeat things like

> Why do you wear your sneakers tied that way—they look ridiculous,

or Stop following leaders. Make up your own dress style,

or You look like a bum.

When your parents nag about your way of dressing, you probably defend yourself or attack them, by saying things like

> You don't know anything about style,

or All the kids wear it. You want me to look like a nerd,

or What about the way you dress.

But instead of defending yourself or attacking, try saying something like

What were the styles like when you were a teenager? Do you have any pictures of the group you used to hang out with? I'd love to see how things were then.

Your parents may pull out some albums and get into talking about the good old days and the crazy ways they dressed and things they did as teens. Before you know it, your parent may realize that he or she also dressed strangely to his or her parents, and that teens' odd dress style is quite normal.

No one likes to admit to being wrong. If you defend yourself or attack your parents, you are in effect saying, "You're wrong. You don't know what you're talking about." But instead, if you get them to realize indirectly that they are wrong, they will let up on you.

Here are some Nevers to keep in mind when it comes to general parental nagging.

- Never look away and act bored
- Never walk away while they are still talking
- Never say "Stop nagging" or "I know all about it,"
- Never, never try to outshout them while they are talking;
- Never verbally attack your parent;
- Never be defensive.

You will find that most parents nag about the same things: curfews, friends, household chores, music, dress and hair, school, sex (boyfriends, girlfriends, etc.), your character (being responsible, honest, etc.), your speech (slang, cursing, vocabulary), and money. Think ahead and plan how you will listen and show understanding for what they are saying. Use an indirect approach to show them the error in their thinking, and finally, plan to take immediate action to right the situation so that your parent will calm down.

All of this may sound suspiciously like giving in, but it is quite the opposite. It is winning by using your intelligence instead of losing by using your emotions. As the renowned psychologist and philosopher William James says, "In an act of will you create something that didn't exist. You can make it happen."[1] Do you really *want* to

[1] Rollo May, *Love and Will* (New York: Dell Publishing Company, 1969), p. 270. May is discussing the philosophy of William James.

change things? Then take the first step by making up your mind that you desire change. This "act of will" can create what does not exist. The moment you decide to change things, something happens. Action follows.

Here is a chart that will help you to take action. If you read the example and then keep a record of your own real-life typical situations, you will develop an awareness of how to change your parents' nagging.

SAMPLE SITUATION

Didn't take out the garbage.

WRONG REACTION
"What's the big deal? You have nothing better to think of than garbage?"

RESULT
Father said, "I'm holding your allowance until you learn to be more responsible."

NEW REACTION
"I should have done it first thing this morning. Sometimes I think I'm the only one with a life. I'll do it right now. I'm sorry."

RESULT
"That's okay, son, you're only human. I forget things, too, sometimes."

TYPICAL SITUATION 1

WRONG REACTION   **RESULT**

NEW REACTION   **RESULT**

TYPICAL SITUATION 2

WRONG REACTION   **RESULT**

NEW REACTION   **RESULT**

TYPICAL SITUATION 3

WRONG REACTION   **RESULT**

NEW REACTION   **RESULT**

4

The Grouch and the Critic

You wonder what's wrong with them. All I did was
ask my mother to move her dress off my newly
ironed shirt. She got mad and started yelling. I was
shocked.

Andrea, *16*

Why do parents sometimes become furious over a minor
thing, when that same offense might provoke just a quiet
comment another time? Why do seemingly odd things get
on their nerves? Why do they sometimes attack your personality—insulting you and putting you down?

If I didn't know better, I'd think my father actually
hated me, the way he talks sometimes.

David, *17*

If you could understand the reason behind your parents' sudden, seemingly irrational, bitter words, you might find some answers to those whys. As a result of your understanding (and maybe even sympathy), they may begin to react differently toward you even when they *are* in a bad mood. Isn't that the goal?

At times, parents are simply down. It could be biorhythms, a bad day at work, or personal pressures. It shouldn't be difficult for you to imagine how a bad day can lead to cutting remarks and impatience. Think of yourself. How do you feel after you miss the bus, get yelled at for not having your math homework, find out your best friend is hanging out with someone else, and learn that you're the only one not invited to the party? When you get home from school, your mother asks you a simple question about when you'd like to go shopping with her for an outfit for your cousin's wedding, and you yell, "Get off my back. Who cares about the———wedding." In a better mood you might simply have said, "Oh, I don't know. Maybe we can go one day this weekend."

In chapter three, I discussed the fact that parents sometimes nag when they have a bad day, but even more often they take out their frustrations by becoming grouchy and critical.

I was in my room listening to the radio at the same loudness I always do. My mother came home from work, and I heard the door slam hard. Right away I knew something was up. A few minutes later she starts yelling, "turn that damn thing down. I can't stand that music." I quickly lowered it before she could come in and start something. When I came out and saw the grouchy look on her face, I grabbed her and gave her a big hug before she could do anything to stop me. Then I gave her a big kiss and said, "I love you, Mom." You should see the way her mood changed—like that.

Deena, *15*

A perfect remedy for a grouchy parent is affection. Parents need lots of love, and unfortunately, they rarely get it from their teenagers. Even dogs need love. If you pet a sad dog, he will wag his tail and start licking you. Affection is a real mood lifter.

The good part is, it's easy to give. All it takes is thirty seconds—a simple hug or a quick kiss on the cheek and an "I love you." We've all heard of the saying "Have you hugged your child today?" Well, how about "Have you hugged your parent this month?"

I interviewed hundreds of parents, asking them what was the best memory they have of their teens—the most happy moment, and every answer related to an affectionate moment.

Tony was only thirteen then. I woke up to find signs all over the house, "Happy Birthday, Dad." Then he served me breakfast in bed. I'll never forget that.

42-year-old father

When Jeannie sent me a card, just like that, no special occasion, telling me how much she appreciates me—the little things I do for her, I was so proud I brought it to work and showed it to everyone.

37-year-old mother of a 16-year-old girl

Alex doesn't usually express himself in a showy way. That's why I couldn't believe it when he gave me this big bear hug and said, "Dad, you're the greatest." It was after we had one of those unexpected talks that really hit home.

40-year-old father of a 17-year-old boy.

I walked into the house and smelled furniture polish. Then I looked around, and the whole house had been cleaned. Tara came out hugging me and yelling, "Surprise." When I asked her why she did it, she said, "Because I love you, Mom." I felt like crying.

You know, just hearing those words meant so much to me. Not that I don't think she loves me, but hearing it means everything. Then you *know*.

41-year-old mother of 14-year-old girl

The small effort can change your parents' moods from down to up. The price of a card, an hour spent cleaning the house or washing the car, or a few seconds taken to say I love you is all that is necessary.

– THE "STOP THAT" GROUCH –

There are times when parents become quite grouchy and it has nothing to do with being in a bad mood. Certain things simply annoy them. For example, some parents can't stand the sound of snapping gum or the clicking of the spoon against a plate. If you think about it, you get annoyed with certain things, too. Jared, a 15-year-old, says,

I can't stand when my brother taps his foot. I mean, it isn't as if he's making noise or anything—it just gets on my nerves. I have to leave the room when he does it. My mother can't understand why it bothers me so much.

If teenagers get annoyed at such little things, imagine how adults, who sometimes have even less tolerance, feel.

The best way to deal with adult quirks is to notice what they are and thus not provoke a bad reaction. Refusing to adjust your behavior will only make you and your parent more frustrated. Jackie, 16, says,

I love to snap my gum. I mean, it's normal. Everyone does it. My mother can't stand it, and she yells, "Get that gum out of your mouth." What's wrong with her anyway. She must be getting old.

Jackie should give in and not chew gum around her mother. Gum snapping is simply not important enough to take a major stand. There are too many other more significant issues Jackie and her mother will have to reach a peace over. Why add this to the list!? Michael could learn a similar lesson.

Sometimes I like to imitate Murdock from *The A Team*. I usually find myself doing it when I'm sitting down waiting for dinner. Whenever I start, my mother goes bananas. "Stop, just stop." I say, "Why, I'm not doing anything wrong." She yells louder, "Look, just stop." I just don't get it.

What if Michael instead said,

Sorry, Mom. I didn't mean to get on your nerves. I'll stop.

His mother would probably calm down and laugh at herself for getting annoyed at such a silly thing. She might say, "I don't know why, but that does drive me mad. Thanks for putting up with my strange ways."

There's no sense in trying to analyze why your parent gets annoyed with certain things. I don't like anyone standing behind my chair. Jared hates the tapping of a foot, and someone else can't stand snapping gum. What should we all do, go to therapy for ten years to discover why? It's much easier to simply give in and stop doing the thing that annoys your parent.

I'm sure your parents do things that get on your nerves, too. Maybe you could make a deal with them. Ask them to exchange lists with you—things that get on your nerves. For example, you might trade off—"I'll stop chomping loudly on my food, Dad, if you stop smoking in the kitchen," or "I'll stop rolling my eyes, Mom, if you stop clearing your throat all the time."

– THE "ARE YOU STUPID?" CRITIC –

Sometimes parents are very critical of you. They insult you when you do something they don't like. For example, you may bring home a bad report card, and your father may say, "What, are you stupid? I have an idiot for a son."

Your father of course doesn't really think you *are* an idiot. What he's really saying is, "I'm afraid I am not doing my job in motivating you to study; then you will be an idiot, and it will be my fault." Most of the time an insult from your parent is really an expression of fear that you will not turn out right and it will be their fault.

Overcome by the feeling they are failing as parents, they forget that what you really need is encouragement and praise, even as you fumble along. Trish, 16, says,

> My father was trying to teach me how to drive. I didn't have control of the brakes, and I kept hitting them hard and the car would lurch. My father kept saying, "No, no, not like that. You'll never learn. What's wrong with you." That made me more nervous, and I kept messing up. I felt like an idiot.

No parent wants to make his or her child feel rejected and insecure. Yet they often don't realize that constant attacks on their children's fumbling efforts to succeed are doing just that. Actually parents who are overly critical feel frustrated that they cannot help their teen succeed at a task. It is really their own seeming failures of which they are most critical! These parents are guilty of impatience and a lack of self-control. They should find a way to stop themselves from making the attacking comments. You can help. I know it's very hard for you to take all of these attacks, even if you do understand why your parents are doing this, but if you try very hard to understand, at least a little bit, it will help.

If your parent attacks you when you are trying something new, perhaps you could say something like

> I know you think I should be learning faster, but I'm really doing the best I can. When you make comments like————I get nervous and I can't think. Then I really mess up. It also makes me think I'm stupid, and I get disgusted. Could you please try to help me, instead of making it harder.

At first your parent might defend him or herself, but I believe most parents would think about these words and later alter their behavior, especially if you remind them every time.

If it doesn't work, then I suggest that the next time your parent asks to teach or show you something, you politely decline and say, "I wish I could let you teach me, but it seems as if every time we try something new, I make a million mistakes. Maybe it's because I get nervous when you make all those comments about how stupid I am. I know you probably don't mean it, but it hurts, and I can't think straight when you do."

Sooner or later, most parents will improve if you keep at them.

In addition to feeling guilty about not doing the job they think they should be doing, your parents can be angry at you for not doing yours. They may be angry with you for being so much trouble, and not the shining example of their creation. Why can't you be easy, they think to themselves. Why can't you learn all the lessons and become an overnight winner? So, out of frustration, they call you names. It's a way of expressing anger.

The fact is, your parents don't mean those names any more than you do when you say, "I hate you" to your mother or father in a moment of rage. What you mean, if you think about it, is you hate what your mother or father is doing to you at that moment. Most wise parents know this. They realize you're not going to get analytical about it and say, "I hate what you're doing to me right now," or "At this moment I feel a surge of hatred toward you because of what you're doing to me." Knowing they're expressing anger, when your parents call you a name or two, don't hold it against them. They're only human. Okay?

Parents readily admit they don't really mean the names they call their teenagers. One mother says,

> I came home and the mayonnaise jar was open, the gas was on, and the meat was all over the table. I said, "You are slow. Something is wrong with your mind." I say that a lot, and I know he hates it. The boy is in honors, and I know he's not slow, but when he does things like that, I can't help but say it.

A father says,

> I find myself calling him a jerk a lot. Every time he does something stupid, I say, "You jerk." One day he got mad and said, "I'm not a jerk." I said, "Then why do you do such stupid things." Later, I thought about it and I said to myself, "I shouldn't be calling him a jerk all the time. Soon he'll believe it."

Well, don't believe it. It's your behavior they really mean to attack, not you.

If you find your parents constantly calling you names, you could reeducate them by calmly restating the name in a more productive way. For example, every time your father calls you stupid, you can say, "You mean that was a stupid thing I did," and so on. If he gets annoyed, it's understandable, but sooner or later he will change his words. You'll wear him down. He'll start catching himself.

Sometimes showing understanding for the way your parent is feeling, and reassuring him or her, works wonders too. Here's what happened when Ray, 16, used this technique.

> Last year I had gotten into a lot of trouble. My father said, "You're going to amount to a big zero." I told him, "Dad, I know I've been a real problem to you, but if you could just put up with me a little longer, I'll get through this in good shape." His whole attitude changed, and he said, "Don't worry, Son. I went through my wild times, too. You'll turn out just fine."

Had Ray argued with his father, "I'm not going to be a zero," his father would probably have given him a list of reasons to prove why he would in fact *be* a loser. More negative feelings would have developed, and nothing would have been accomplished. *The easy thing to do is defend yourself. The intelligent thing to do is to say something to comfort your distraught parent.*

– THE "WHY CAN'T YOU BE GOOD" CRITIC –

Sometimes parents criticize your appearance because they are embarrassed by it. Sal's father called him a mental case when he walked in with a Mohawk haircut.

> I came in with the haircut, and my father started flipping out. He called me everything you could name and said he wouldn't be seen in the street with me, much less my cousin's Bas Mitzvah. He ended up calling me a mental case.

Sal, *15*

What Sal's father is really afraid of is that people will think *he* is a mental case for letting his son get that haircut.

Denine's mother seems to suffer from a similar fear of what people will think of her.

The last time I called her a slut was when we were going to visit some relatives in New Jersey. She had on so much makeup, and that tight dress way above her knees. You'd think she was going to Forty-second Street. How could I walk in to my sister's house with my own daughter looking that way. When I tell her about it, she says I don't know anything about the styles nowadays.

43-year-old mother— (Denine, *16*)

I think that both Sal and Denine should have some consideration for their parents. Sal could have waited until after the Bas Mitzvah to get the haircut, and Denine could modify her dress for family occasions. Compromise can go a long way toward creating peace and harmony at home. You give in a little, and your parents will be grateful and back off a little.

Teenagers tell me that they want to "be themselves," and that by changing their makeup, hair or dress just to suit their parents for an occasion, they are being "phony." They miss the point. It's not being phony, it's being mature. A wise person evaluates each situation and modifies his or her behavior to suit that particular occasion. When you are sure of yourself, of who you are, you will not be threatened by changing your appearance to suit a need—for a day or so. Sometimes it takes more strength to give in than it does to fight for your "cause." Think about it.

– "I CAN'T BELIEVE MY PARENTS THINK I'M UNPLEASANT!" –

One of the biggest causes of parents being grouchy and critical is, believe it or not, teenagers being grouchy and criticl first. One mother says,

> I was in a great mood. I mean, the sun was shining, I had had a good day, and I was looking good. I was driving my daughter, Kate, to her dance lesson, and I said, "How was your day?" She didn't answer. A few seconds later I said, "You look very pretty today." She barely nodded. Then I said, "I'm really making progress on my diet. Everyone is telling me I look like I'm losing weight." She said, "Yeah, yeah, Mom. That's nice." That's when I exploded. I called her a self-centered prima donna. I said things like "All you ever think about is yourself." By the time we got to the dance studio, I just said, "Get out." I drove away feeling pretty low. I thought, "What should I do. Not talk to her?"

Parents don't know when it changed, but they know something did. Their children used to be so pleasant, but now that they are teens, they can rarely get a civil comment out of them. I asked one 14-year-old if she is often nasty to her parents even when they are being nice to her. She said,

> Yes. My father will be so polite and try to make polite conversation. I'm just grouchy with him. He says, "Why can't you be pleasant." I say, "I don't want to be pleasant." Then he walks away in a huff.

A while ago people were wearing small buttons that said, Smile. It's Contagious. Well, grouchiness and criticism are also contagious. If you want your parent to be nasty, then just keep on being unpleasant. Even a saint will curse you out if you press the right button. On the other hand, if you want to create a pleasant, sunny atmosphere for yourself, then make an effort to be civil, and even cheerful, to your parent. Force yourself to answer questions and engage in conversation. Life at home will be far more pleasant.

Had Kate answered her mother's question about her day, said, "Thank you," for the compliment, and had the courtesy to make a few encouraging comments about her mother's diet, the argument never would have happened. Kate would have undoubtedly had much nicer thoughts as she began her dance lesson, and her mother may not have had to leave the scene wondering how she could cope with living with this "monster."

If you think about it, when you argue with your parents, very often that negative mood carries over to other things. You arrive at school and get into an argument with a teacher. Before you know it, you're being given a penalty of some sort. Then you argue with your boyfriend or girlfriend. All of this can be avoided if you learn to be pleasant and use a little self-control. You know you can do it if you want to.

Some parents will even say "I hate you" if driven to it. A 39-year-old mother of a 14-year-old girl says:

It was early in the morning and we were both in a hurry trying to get ready for going out. I'm always so pleasant in the morning, but she's death warmed over. I asked her a simple question, "Where's the hair spray?" She answered in a nasty tone, "How should I know." Then I asked her if she wanted breakfast. She said, "Leave me alone. Can't you see I'm in a hurry." Then I went into the bathroom and found the towels bunched up on the floor. I asked her to hang them up. She said, "Get off my back." I walked into my room muttering "I hate you,' and she heard me. She said, "I heard that." Defending myself I said, "Yes. I do hate you. It's hell living with you..." And I said a lot of other things, too. Later I felt so guilty. I don't hate her. I love her. It's just so frustrating sometimes. I don't know how to handle her. Is this the way all teenagers are or did I just get stuck with an extra moody one?

If your mother or father has ever said "I hate you," or the equivalent, remember—your parents don't hate you any more than you hate your parents when you say "I hate you" or even just think it. It's just the rage of the frustrating moment that is talking. What your parents really hate is the treatment you are giving him or her . . . not you.

Here are some things to remember when dealing with grouchy or critical parents:

1. Remember to express affection in words or deeds as often as possible. Your parents are starved for love.

2. Show compassion and understanding for what they are going through. Get them talking about their lives and sympathize with them.

3. Find opportunities to give your parents an honest compliment. Everyone loves a compliment.

4. Remember to say thank you. Show appreciation for all the little things they do for you. "Thank you for driving me . . ." etc.

5. Ask questions about their life when they were teenagers.

6. Help your parents to rephrase their attack by saying, "You mean I did a stupid thing. . . ." etc.

7. Be pleasant and courteous yourself. Grouchiness and criticism are as contagious as smiles and compliments.

Here are some "nevers" to remember when dealing with grouchy or critical parents.

1. Never say, "What's the matter. Did you have a bad day and you're taking it out on me?"

2. Never continue to do an annoying thing because you think it shouldn't annoy them.

3. Never believe for one moment that your parents really think *you* are the name they call you. They're just frustrated and angry.

4. Never leave the house angry with your parents. Make up. Apologize for being grouchy. Admit when you are wrong. You'll have a better day.

Here is a chart that will help you to use some of the information discussed in this chapter. Remember to keep track of your more positive responses.

SAMPLE SITUATION

Failed a math test and father called me an idiot.

WRONG REACTION
"So what? I hate math anyway."

RESULT
We argued and he threatened to ground me.

NEW REACTION
"I'm not an idiot. I just didn't study hard enough. I'll have to crack those books. I can do it."

RESULT
"I think you can, too. It frustrates me when I know you don't study and I see grades like this."

TYPICAL SITUATION

WRONG REACTION

RESULT

NEW REACTION

RESULT

TYPICAL SITUATION

WRONG REACTION   **RESULT**

NEW REACTION   **RESULT**

TYPICAL SITUATION

WRONG REACTION   **RESULT**

NEW REACTION   **RESULT**

5

I'm Not a Baby or a Criminal

You wait for the big day when you're eighteen, so you can have your freedom. Then you get the speech: "Just because you're eighteen doesn't mean you can do anything you want. As long as you're living under this roof..."

Lydia, 18

Chances are, your parents are a bit too overprotective. They try to get you to dress warmly, take your medicine, remember your key, and "be careful." They may bombard you with hundreds of questions about your personal life, hoping to find out if you are staying on "the right track." You may be the only one in your group with an early curfew, and your parents may demand that you call them even if you're going to be five minutes late.

Is there any hope for changing such parental behavior? The answer is yes.

Your parents will always worry about you and will in some ways always yearn to supervise your life. It is a by-product of their love. The critical issue, however, is degree. As the years go by, you will naturally want them to become less involved in the details of your life. So, your goal should be to help your parents to slowly loosen their grip on the controls. This is healthy for them as well as for you.

As a teenager, your job is to become gradually more and more independent. The only problem is, your parents find it very difficult to let go. They are used to having to protect you. After all, what would have happened if they didn't keep a watchful eye on you as you were growing up. You may have been hit by a car, kidnapped, or worse. Years ago they had to be sure you were dressed properly for school, and they were indeed wise to keep a close watch on the friends you stayed with. Your parents know they can't keep doing such things forever—No parent thinks he or she will be telling you who to have as a friend when you are thirty years old—it's just that they think the time to stop is later. Never *now*. Unfortunately, your parents' inclinations are exactly the opposite of what you might feel you need.

Dr. Daniel Offer, an expert on adolescent psychology, says that adolescence presents you with a special burden. You have to establish self-confidence and learn to make important decisions concerning your future. You have to free yourself from your childhood attachment to your parents.[1] Can you see the problem? Here you are, trying to do the healthy, normal, "growing up" task of moving away from the dependency on your parents, and here they are, taking your efforts to move away as an insult—fighting you every step of the way.

But wait a minute. Your parents are not *all* wrong.

[1]Dr. Daniel Offer, M.D., "Adolescent Turmoil," *New York University Quarterly*, (Winter 1982): p. 31. Landmarks in Literature.

They know that you can't wake up one morning and suddenly be wise enough to completely make all decisions for yourself. They're afraid you will make serious mistakes and that harm will come to you. At times they see things that you don't see, and in their wisdom they step in and lay down rules to stop you from hurting yourself. At the time you are furious about it, but in the end you look back and see that they were right. But other times they are wrong. They are still thinking that you are the child they miss—the child that depended completely upon them. They liked those "good old days," and don't want them to end.

The problem is clear. Your parents are right in trying to protect you—and yet they are wrong in protecting you too much. Just as you are learning to be independent and making mistakes along the way; they are learning how much to let go and committing their own errors. They are, in a sense, experimenting with you as they go along. Even if they had the experience with your older brothers or sisters (it helps a little), they still have to experience letting go of *you*. Every teenager is different.

If you understand how hard it is for them, and if you learn to help them to let go by showing understanding, you will find that the fighting and anger will be much less bitter and that your life will run smoothly.

If you confront your parents head-on and say something like:

You treat me like a ten-year-old. Why don't you wake up. I'm sixteen years old. All my friends...

You can be sure your parents will come back with good reasons why they are right and you and all of your friends' parents are wrong. If, on the other hand, you use a little psychology and show a little understanding for their concerns, you may just see them relax a little and let go of the reins a bit. Remember, they won't (and shouldn't) suddenly let go and give you complete freedom. You're looking for degrees—slow, sure progress.

My daughter used a little psychology on me and it worked. She was thirteen years old and had asked if she could go to a roller rink on Fridays from 8:00 to 11:00 with all of her friends. I said no, pointing out that I didn't care if all her friends were allowed to go. One Friday she was staying over a girlfriend's house and I happened to call her at 9:00. The girl's mother told me that she had driven them to the rink and would be picking them up at 11:00. Naturally I was angry and was planning to punish my daughter.

The next day I told my daughter I knew about her going behind my back and that I was planning a good punishment. While I was stewing in the living room, she was busily composing this letter, which she handed to me twenty minutes later.

Mom,
I'm sorry about last night. I shouldn't have gone behind your back, but all my friends or most of them go, and it's like I have nothing to do but stay home. All I want to do is hang out and have a good time with my friends. A while ago you said that if I went, I would see how bad the place was, but it was fun and not bad at *all*. I can understand your fears, but if I go with five or six friends and someone drops us off and picks us up, it isn't so bad. But I do understand your fear. There are no shady characters at the rink.

P.S. Please try to understand my growing up is not as bad as it seems.

You must be wondering, what's so great about that letter. Well, from a parent's point of view, it's irresistible. You see, my daughter put her finger right on the real problem in her P.S. I was having a real struggle with her growing up. It was hard for me to take the next step and let her have so much time away, unsupervised. And yet I knew she must be given this freedom sooner or later.

Another great thing about the letter is its pointing out that she understands my fears. This is very important for you to do for your parents. If you show them that you are aware of the very real dangers out there, they will feel more confident to let you take your chances. They will be reassured that you are alert and looking out for yourself.

Finally, her specifically talking about the fears and showing me that I have no real reason to worry helped. She was calm, logical, and kind. And it was in a letter. I didn't have to confront her, and there was no chance for me to argue with her.

The end result is, I found myself being one of the mothers driving and picking up on Friday nights.

Your parents may drive you to the point of almost hating them because of the way they try to control your life.

> They don't understand I'm a person. They tell me what to do all the time, but don't they know that whatever I do, I'm the one that will have to live with it?
>
> *Tracy, 16*

Tracy is a bit wrong. You see, whatever you do, your parents will also have to live with it—live with the pain of knowing that they could have, should have, saved you. Remember, they are always afraid that they are not being perfect or good enough parents.

> They ask you so many questions, you'd think you were being arrested for a crime.
>
> *Gina, 15*

But think of it this way. Your parents really care. Maybe you can forgive them if you realize that the reason your parents intrude on your life so much is their love for you. If they didn't care, they would be thrilled to see you stay

out all the time—away—out of their hair. They would
be free to enjoy their own lives. Parents don't enjoy constantly watching over you. It is hard work for them. They'd
love to be free of the responsibility, but their love for you
won't let them.

— "MY SEX LIFE IS
MY DECISION" —

Parents tend to intrude on you when it comes to your
relationship with the opposite sex.

My mother thinks I spend too much time with my
boyfriend. She believes you start dating seriously
when you're nineteen and then you marry that boy.
She says I should have more than one boyfriend.
She tries to tell me how to feel. I wish she'd stop
treating me like a baby.

Sherry, 15

Sherry's first reaction may be to tell her mother that
times have changed. Today's teenagers have lots of
"steady" relationships that don't lead to marriage. She
might then say things like "You don't know what's happening," or "Don't tell me how to feel. You just don't
understand me."
In response, her mother would naturally defend herself
and say things like "I know more than you think I do.
You spend enough time with that boy, and before you
know it, you'll be pregnant."
Sherry and her mother would both be better served by
a different conversation. It did not help Sherry to confront
her mother with insults indicating that she's not up on the
times and pointing out that she is failing as a mother and
simply doesn't understand her own daughter. Sherry must
put her anger and her ego aside and think about what is

going on in her mother's mind. Then speak.

First she must realize that her mother is afraid she will become too involved with a boy if she sees only that one boy and that behind this fear is fear of sexual involvement. Sherry's goal must be to bring her mother's fear out into the open and reassure her by indicating that she, too, is aware of this possibility and has it under control. She could say something like

A lot of girls my age are getting pregnant. I don't know what kind of understanding they have, but I'm too smart for that. All the talks we had didn't go in vain, you know. I like [Joe] a lot, but we're not doing anything. Don't worry, Mom. It's just not my personality to have more than one boyfriend at a time. Some girls do, but I'm too busy to handle more than one.

This approach would at least help Sherry's mother to talk about her fears. Her mother might say, "Are you sure you're not getting in too deep?" Sherry could reassure her some more, and Sherry's mother could let go, just a little.

One other important thing to do when reassuring your parents is to let them know (as I suggest Sherry do) that their lectures have been getting through to you. Tell your parents that you have been listening to them and understand their values. Parents are not mind readers. Sometimes they imagine you don't hear a word they say and so worry that when you go out into the cruel world you'll be defenseless. Try to think of their favorite theme of warnings. Write down the message they are trying to get across. Then you can express it back to them in similar words. It will relieve them and make them happy to see that they have not been talking to the wall. For example, if your parent is always saying, "You're known by the company you keep," you might let him or her know that there are certain groups in school that you stay away from because you realize that people do influence you.

– "I THINK I CAN CHOOSE
MY OWN FRIENDS" –

Your parents are afraid that if your friends do drugs,
you will do drugs. If your friends cut school, so will you.
If they vandalize and steal, so will you. You know that
some of your friends do things that you wouldn't do, and
you know that you've stopped hanging out with certain
people because you realize these people could somehow
get you into trouble. But your parents don't know that
you have such wisdom. Without being defensive, let them
know you are a good judge of character.

The best way to handle parental prying when it comes
to friends is to stop being so secretive. Let them meet
your friends. Talk openly to them about your friends. If
some friends do have a problem, discuss that problem
with your parents. Dare to tell them about friend X, who
is smoking a lot of pot these days. Talk about friend Y,
who has been failing in school. Ask your parents for advice
on how to encourage your friend to stop cutting his classes.
Your parents will be impressed that you have a mind of
your own and that you are a good influence on your friends.
They may still feel uneasy about your spending too much
time with these problem friends, but they will relax their
pull on you a great deal because they'll know you have
a good head on your shoulders and that you want to come
out on top—a winner.

I used to bring my friends home and ask my father in
advance to study them. I'd say, "I'm bringing my friend
John around. I want to know what you think he's all about.
Try to get him talking to you."

After John left, he would give me his analysis. The
funny thing is, he was usually right in his assessment. He
would point out that so-and-so was a bit shy and a bit
shifty—secretive, and that this one was fun loving and
open-minded and intelligent. In the long run, I agreed with
him, it made him feel involved, and it kept him off my
back about certain people. I was able, on my own, to drop

certain friends and make new ones. My parents left it to me.

– "I WANT TO LOOK LIKE ME, NOT YOUR VERSION OF ME" –

In their desire to make sure you look your best, some parents try to push their opinion on you when you buy clothes.

> Every time I go shopping with my mother, she pushes her ideas on me. I wanted a royal-blue coat, but she kept saying, "the gray-black is smarter." I finally gave in and got it, but I never really liked it.
>
> *Sandy, 14*

Parents do this because they see you as their creation—their little doll, so to speak. Naturally they have their own ideas as to what looks best and it kills them when you refuse to let them dress you—the way they used to—to suit the perfect image. It's hard for them to realize they have to let go and allow you to dress yourself, even if they don't like the end result.

If you have a problem in this area, the best thing you can do is to have an open heart-to-heart with your parents. Sandy could say something like

> Mom, I know you think the gray-black is smarter, and maybe it is. But I love the royal-blue. It reflects my personality,   or
>
> I have to begin finding my own style. Do you think you could manage to look away and let me start making my own decisions when it comes to my clothing,   or
>
> I love your taste, but we have different personalities. If I get the gray-black, I won't feel happy

when I wear it. Didn't that ever happen to you— you didn't get the one you really liked, and then you never enjoyed the thing?

You owe it to yourself to do your job. You must become independent and let go of your parents, and part of your job is to help your parents let go of you. You have to actually teach your parents that it is time for them to let you make your own choices—even if those choices are quite different from what they would choose.

If the above brief exchanges don't work, Sandy could be even more specific. She could set some time aside later for a lengthier talk. Then she could gently tell her mother that some day she will have to make her own choices, develop her own taste, so she would like to start in small steps. Now is a good time, isn't it?

I remember the first time my daughter refused to let me comb her hair for a family occasion. It was Thanksgiving, and all of my relatives would be there. She insisted on creating this hairstyle that to me made her look mousy and unattractive. I like to show off my daughter's beautiful blond hair. It killed me to let her be when she said, "When are you going to let me comb my own hair?" She was ten years old at the time. I thought to myself, "She's right. The day must come when I let her comb her own hair."

Think of it. Each little step of independence is something new for your parents. You did not enter their lives equipped with a manual, unlike their car. They have to figure out what to do, on their own, every step of the way. That's why you have to help.

Parents are experimenting, trial and error. By name calling you will only make them hold tighter. By gently helping them to let go, you will gain gradual freedom.

– "WHY CAN'T I STAY OUT LATER?" –

A favorite and very understandable area of parental overprotection is curfews. Your parents are scared to death that something will happen to you. They imagine your being mugged, in a car accident, in a fight, and on and on. For this reason they try to keep a tight reign on your whereabouts. If you are late, the wheels of their mind begin to turn and they go through hell. Probably the worst kind of torture you can put your parents through is to be more than a little late and not let them know where you are.

> I was two hours late. When I got in the door, my mother went crazy. "Where were you. I was just about to call the police. You're punished for a month." I was going to call, but I knew she would make me come home. I was having such a good time at the party I figured I'd make up a story when I got home. Damn. I was only two hours late. Not two weeks.
>
> *Annie, 16*

Annie didn't call because she wanted to be sure to stay at the party. She wasn't thinking about her parents. Had she thought about their fears, she might have been more considerate and called.

A 42-year-old mother of a 14-year-old says

> You'd think I'd learn. It's almost embarrassing. My daughter said she would be leaving her friend's house at eleven o'clock and would be home about eleven-fifteen. The girl lives five blocks away, but it's not the best neighborhood. She promised that if her plans changed and she left the girl's house earlier, she would call. At eleven-thirty she still wasn't home, so I called the girl's house. "Oh, she left at ten," I was told. I hung up the phone and felt my whole body tighten up. I pictured her walking home and

someone grabbing her into a car. I called her other girlfriend, hoping she stopped there. When the girl said she didn't hear from her, I could hardly control my voice. Tears were coming. I said, "Thank you," and hung up. I jumped in the car and drove around for ten minutes. When I got home, I thought, surely she'll be there. I called her name, but no one answered. I started to pray. "Oh, God. Please help me. If only she's all right." I was just about to call one of her friends and ask her to cruise the neighborhood for all possible places she might walk. Just then the door opened. Now it was eleven thirty-five. She was smiling and happy. I started screaming, "Where were you. You weren't at Jennifer's house. You promised to call if . . ." She said, "Oh, I forgot to call. I went over to Rob's house." "Do you see what time it is," I said. She looked at the clock and said casually, "Oh, I must have lost track of the time." The night ended up with my working myself up into a rage and announcing punishments and her crying woefully in her room and mumbling, "I hate you." Later, I thought, What should I do. Just not worry no matter what she does? But I knew I was fooling myself. Who knows? One time she might really be in trouble. I'll have to live this way until she grows into an adult.

This story is typical. I've spoken to hundreds of parents. It may be hard for you to imagine because you're out having such a good time. You *know* you are safe, so you think they shouldn't worry. But they don't know what's going on.

Have a heart. Your parents really worry about you because they love you so much. If you want to be late, call and say, "I'm having such a good time. Please let me stay another hour or two." If they say no, you can say, okay, I'll be home soon. Or if you feel you *must* stay, then in another hour call again and say, I'm leaving now. You'll probably still be punished but not as severely. And at least you'll know you didn't take a few years off their lives.

– "I FEEL LIKE I'M IN JAIL" –

But what do you do about parents who are too strict, and who give you ridiculous limits?

I'm the only one in my crowd that has to be home so early on a weekend night. If we are all hanging out at someone's house on a Friday, I have to leave at ten-thirty. Everyone else stays till twelve or one o'clock. My father says, "You should be glad I let you go at all." He just doesn't understand.

Carey, 15

Some parents are too strict. I'll admit it. Why? Perhaps it is because their parents were very strict with them. Also, you may be an only child or the oldest—the first teenager they have to deal with. Whatever the root cause, your parents are being strict because they are afraid that something will happen to you if they don't keep a tight reign on you. The only way you can help them to loosen the reigns is to show that you are responsible. You have to earn their trust. Carey might try to convince her parents to let her stay out until 11:30, one hour later than usual, by inviting her mother to speak with the parent who will be home while the teenagers are there. Encouraging your mother to speak with other mothers helps, especially if you don't approach the situation as an attack on your mother—implying that she doesn't know what's going on and she needs other mothers to tell her how to be a good parent.

You could talk with your friends' parents and explain your situation. Ask one or two of your friends' mothers to call your house and casually get into a conversation about their teenagers. You could have this parent bring up the subject of how hard it is to know what the limits are. She could talk openly with your mother about how she sets limits and why those limits (a little more liberal than yours) seem fine for teenagers your age. If one or two mothers do this, and handle it diplomatically, your mother will relax her rigid standard. She'll probably be relieved to have others to talk to, and she won't feel so guilty about giving you more freedom. Many times parents are strict because they fear giving you too much freedom. That would make them in their own minds careless parents. Speaking with other parents would give them backups, and in their minds they would think, "Well, these other mothers seem to be quite responsible, and they think it's okay, so I guess it is."

Whatever you do, don't ever say things like, "Talk to Mrs.——— She lets . . ." or "You're the only one . . ." This might cause your mother to put up a huge defense ahead of time, and then when the other mothers call, she will be very suspicious and unable to listen. She will feel obliged to defend her position. Use self-control. Work behind the scenes.

Another reason many parents are overly strict with curfews is the simple fact that they can't relax until you are home safe, and this means they lose precious sleep waiting up for you. If this is the case, encourage them to set an alarm clock and place it outside their bedroom door, set for ten to twenty minutes after your curfew time. Tell them to go to sleep and that when you come home, you will turn off the clock. If you are late, of course you can't get to the clock, so they will wake up. This will take care of their not allowing you a later curfew just on the basis of "It's too late for me to stay up waiting. I need my sleep."

Your parents may also feel they should stay home, putting aside their own fun, so that they can be sure you come home safe. Strict curfews give them a bit more free time.

If your parents want to go out, suggest that they call the house around the time that you are supposed to be home. In addition, give them the telephone numbers of places you will be if you are not home at the expected time. Also, get the phone number of places they will be so that if you're going to be late, you can call them.

Another idea if your parents are going to be out is to leave a message on the answering machine if you are going to be late. If your parents have a machine and a beeper, they might call in and receive the message from the machine, saying not to worry and you'll be home at X o'clock. You'll explain later. At least this would free your parents to go out and have fun without worrying about you, and it would show that you are responsible.

Sometimes teenagers incur the suspicion of parents who used to trust them because they did something to lose that trust. Once your parents catch you doing something wrong, they may treat you as if you were a criminal for a long time after. One mother says,

> It took me about seven months to trust Sally again. She told me she was sleeping over a friend's house, and I happened to call there. The other mother knew nothing about it. The next day Sally came home acting like nothing was wrong. I told her I knew, and she admitted to going to an all-night party. I know she's seventeen, but it gave me the creeps to think that she was one place while I thought she was in another.

The only way to win back trust is to prove yourself again. Apologize for lying, and don't defend the lie. Tell your parents that there was no excuse for your behavior and that you know what you did was wrong and you don't blame them for not trusting you. Tell them that you want to win back their trust, and ask them if they will give you a chance to do it. Then be patient, and tolerate their suspicions for a little while. Let them check up on you. It's only natural. Instead of getting angry, understand. Leave a phone number whenever it is possible, letting them know where you'll be. Leave them a few numbers if you'll be moving around. Just this effort will underline your desire to be responsible. If you hang in there, trust will return and things will be on an even keel again.

Once you betray a trust, you may have to pay the price for a while. Jose, 17, says,

> I was in my room getting high and my mother started banging on the door. I think she smelled the aroma. I started playing with the lock, trying to buy time and hoping that the smell would go out the window. She knew, and I admitted what I was doing. Now every time I lock my door she comes around yelling, "What are you doing in there?" What a pain.

If Jose had an honest talk with his mother and admitted that he doesn't blame her for checking up on him, and if he asked her to give him a chance to prove himself, his mother might be less offensive in her "checks." She might be more sensitive to Jose's feelings and might at times give him the benefit of the doubt. In any case, if you've done something to betray your parents trust, remember that it will take time to win it back, but if you speak to them, they may help you to win it back by giving a little trust to you while you are working on it.

In general, parents feel that every once in a while they should check up on you—just because that is what good parents are supposed to do. They may periodically call the school to check up on your attendance, casually pass by in a car (where you hang out), call the home of a friend looking for you pretending to ask you something (but really checking to see if you are where you said you would be), strain to smell your breath when you come home from a party, stare deeply into your eyes trying to see signs of your being high on drugs. Don't be insulted. They hear so much about teenagers doing all sorts of things that they worry about you. They're afraid that things could be happening right under their very noses.

So if you feel at times as if you're being checked up on as if you were a criminal, understand. Your parents are covering all the bases because they want so much to make sure you turn out all right.

The next time you find out that your parent checked up on you, instead of becoming indignant and outraged, try this. Tell your parent, "I see you've been checking up on me again. I see I can't put anything over on you, not that I'd want to. At first I was annoyed and embarrassed when I found out you did that, but after I thought about it, I said to myself, it's because they care about me."

If you got the message of this chapter, the above statements won't be "phony." And your parents will feel relieved to know that you appreciate their efforts. The best part is they will check up less because they will see that you know they check up. Everyone will be happier.

In review, here are some very important Dos and Don'ts in dealing with parents who are overprotective or who tend to treat you as if you were a criminal.
Do remember the following:

1. Show understanding for what your parent is going through in letting you become more independent.

2. Show that you are aware of the real dangers in the world.

3. Show that you have been absorbing their lectures and values.

4. Ask their opinion as often as possible.

5. Let them meet and talk to your friends.

6. Have a heart-to-heart talk about letting you make your own decisions regarding clothing, hairstyle, etc.

7. Let them talk to other more liberal parents if they are too strict by having other parents casually start the conversation.

8. Always call when you'll be more than a little late.

9. Be patient if you've done something to lose their trust. Ask them to help you to win it back.

10. Understand that they should be doing some checking. It is a parent's job to be sure that you are on the right track.

Here are some very important Nevers.

1. Never confront your overprotective parent head-on by saying, for example, "You treat me like a ten-year-old."

2. Never say, "It's my life." It's their life, too.

3. Never say, "Times have changed. You don't know what's happening."

4. Never say, "Everyone else is allowed."

5. Never give up. If you keep working on them, they will find the courage to loosen their grip and trust you.

Here is a chart that will help you to use some of the information gained in this chapter. Read the example, and then keep a record of your own experiences.

SAMPLE SITUATION

Mother called attendance office checking my record.

WRONG REACTION
I called her a spy.

RESULT
Argument.

NEW REACTION
"I see you're right on the case, Ma. Now you know how good I've been lately."

RESULT
Mother laughed and said, "I'm glad to see I was wasting my money for the phone call."

TYPICAL SITUATION

WRONG REACTION   **RESULT**

NEW REACTION   **RESULT**

TYPICAL SITUATION

WRONG REACTION   **RESULT**

NEW REACTION   **RESULT**

TYPICAL SITUATION

WRONG REACTION   **RESULT**

NEW REACTION   **RESULT**

6

It Was So Embarrassing!

What's the most embarrassing thing your parents did to you? Did they reprimand you in front of friends, yell at you in a public place, wear a ridiculous outfit, start dancing in front of your friends, or start telling dumb jokes? Maybe your parents always want you to take a walk to or go out to eat in a place where all your friends hang out. Why do parents do embarrassing things to teenagers and what can you do to stop them?

– "I CAN'T BELIEVE IT WHEN THEY YELL AT ME IN PUBLIC" –

Many times parents don't realize how humiliating their actions can be. They simply react to the moment. Recently

I attended a barbecue where a group of teenagers were hanging out on one side of the yard, while the adults stayed together on the other. A 15-year-old girl came over to the table where I was sitting to talk to her mother. At that moment a new group of teenagers arrived, and one of them said to the 15-year-old girl, "We had a good time last night." One thing led to another, and as it turned out, the mother of the 15-year-old had forbidden her to have company when she wasn't home. It was clear her daughter had violated that rule. In front of everyone, the mother yelled, "You are grounded, young lady." She then proceeded to lecture her daughter about the proper way to behave. The poor girl's face turned bright red. Looking as if she were fighting tears, she lowered her head. Finally she walked away.

I was so furious with the mother that at first I didn't trust myself to speak with her, but then I calmed down when it occurred to me, "Here's a chance to learn something." I wondered what on earth would make a mother want to humiliate her own daughter in public that way. I asked the woman, "Why did you yell at your daughter in front of all those people? She looked as if she would cry any minute." Still seething, the mother said, "She deceived me and I am furious. I was angry, and I don't care who's around." I asked her if she didn't think it would have been better to wait to talk to her daughter in private, and her answer was, "I can't wait. I'm too angry."

Let's face it. Sometimes parents can't or won't control their anger, and you have to pay the price of being embarrassed. It isn't that they plan to hurt you, it's just that they are human, they have bad days, and they do have tempers. I'm sure the mother would agree it would have been better to reprimand her daughter later, but she simply didn't have the self-control to do that.

Parents do things in the heat of the moment and are sorry for it later. Here's what happened to Frankie.

My father doesn't like my wasting my money on video games, and I promised him I wouldn't play them. He was passing by the pizza place where I hang out and play video games, and he saw me. Before I could jump away and pretend I was eating pizza, he came in and grabbed me by the arm and pulled me out, right in front of these two girls that go to my school. I thought to myself, I'll never show my face in school again.

Frankie, 13

The story has an interesting ending.

When I got home, I locked my room and my father and my brother were talking. My brother must have made him see how wrong he was, because he apologized and said, "I know I shouldn't have come in and embarrassed you that way. It's just that I got so mad when I saw you there playing; you promised..."

Parents do have tempers, but sometimes they do admit their mistakes. If Frankie's father and the fifteen-year-old girl's mother don't admit their mistakes, perhaps they could be approached in this way.

You know, I understand how angry you must have been when... but I wish you would have spoken to me in private. I was so embarrassed. Didn't you ever have that happen to you... when your mother or father did something that made you die of embarrassment...

Most parents remember their own embarrassing teen experiences. If you can get them to talk about it, the end result would be more sensitive, aware parents; parents that might find a bit more self-control the next time they are tempted to give vent to wild anger.

– "WHAT WILL EVERYONE THINK?" –

Quite often parents unwittingly embarrass you in front of your friends. Your mother may call you loudly in for dinner when you're outside with a bunch of friends, or she may try to joke around with your friends in a way that makes you cringe. All they are doing is being themselves, but you could die a million deaths. Stacey, 15, says,

> When my friends came over, my mother said, "Why don't you fumigate your room before you let others inside." My friends laughed, but I think they must wonder about her.

I asked one mother why she likes to joke around with her daughter's friends. She says,

> I love to have an audience. Her friends seem to get a kick out of me. Teenagers are a snap. I love to joke with them.

Parents get tired of being boring. They want to have some fun, too. Jared can't see the humor in his father's attempt to joke around. He says,

> My father and I were in the store buying some soda. When the man gave my father the soda can, my father asked him to wipe off the top of the can. The man said, "The can is clean." My father said, "There may have been roaches crawling on it." Now the store was clean. I could have died, so I walked away and pretended I didn't know him.

Jared, Stacey, and every other embarrassed teenager imagines that there is an audience watching them. They believe that people are thinking, "What a jerk his or her mother or father is." They also imagine that people are thinking that they must be stupid or retarded having such imbeciles for parents. But think of this: people are probably mildly amused by the joke. They are thinking about their own lives, and you are the last thing on their minds. They have their own problems. Still, this is not much comfort when the embarrassing moment takes place in front of someone you know well....

One way to understand what people really think when a parent does something embarrassing is to remember how you feel when your friends' parents do something that drives him or her crazy. Sometimes you think nothing of it at all. You may even wonder why your friend is embarrassed! Simone, 14, says,

> You know, the funny thing is, if someone else's mother or father does something, you laugh it off, but if it's your own mother or father, you think everyone is looking at you. I'm starting to realize that and not get so embarrassed anymore.

Parents want to have fun. Sometimes this can get embarrassing.

> My mother, sister, and I went to the zoo. Suddenly my mother started jumping and skipping in circles. I said, "Mommy, calm down; people are looking." She yells out, "I'm not Mommy, I'm sister." Then she ran up the stairs and stopped on one foot and looked like she was getting ready to fly. My sister and I looked at each other as if to say...
>
> *Shiela, 16*

Shiela's mother wants to feel young again. Maybe while at the zoo, she suddenly remembered her childhood days. It made her feel carefree and foolish, and so she wanted to be "sister," and not "mother." Is she crazy? No. She's normal. As hard as it may be for you to accept this fact, parents are sometimes really very young at heart, and they get very bored with acting "straight," the way they are "supposed to act." I hope you're not boring when you become a parent.

Sometimes parents drink too much or even get high. This really upsets teenagers.

> My father gets high, and then he starts bugging out in front of my friends. He makes an ass of himself.
>
> *Craig, 17*

> My mother started drinking at the party we had for my birthday. All my friends were there, and she was doing these crazy dances acting all wild and stupid. I was so ashamed of her I wanted to hide her in a closet.
>
> *Janet, 16*

Janet and Craig could talk to their parents about proper parental behavior. They could give their parents a lecture about how good parents should always behave, but my guess is the parent will become indignant and demand the right to have some fun, too.

If your parents embarrass you by acting foolish in public, you could have a talk with them about how you feel. This would make them aware, and they would try to cool it a little. Then you would not be embarrassed as often. But please, give them a break. Your parents aren't going to be very comfortable if they have to watch every move around you. One mother says,

> I was driving my daughter and two of her friends to the movies. I started singing and snapping my fingers. My daughter said, "Please, Mom, don't sing." I stopped, but I was annoyed. I thought, "I can't wait until I drop them off so I can sing in peace, if I wish."

Try to understand, your parent wants to enjoy life, too. And remember, your friends are probably thinking nothing of it. It's mainly in your mind.

Some things are understandably embarrassing, although they may completely mystify your parents. One of the biggest mysteries to many parents is the one regarding teenagers' unwillingness to be seen in front of their friends with a parent. Sari, a 16-year-old, says,

My father wants me to take a walk with him. If my friends see me walking around with my father, what will they think? I try to explain, but he just doesn't understand. Nobody takes walks with their father.

The best way to remedy situations like this one is to find other time to spend alone with your parent. Your parents want to "take a walk" or "go out to eat" not for the express purpose of parading around with you in front of your friends, but to be alone with you and to have a talk. Your parent is hoping to get to know you better, to find a way to get close to you. Parents sense the changes taking place in their children who are no longer children, and they are desperately trying to find ways to keep a relationship going. If you don't want to take a walk with your parent, why not suggest something else, like a car ride to a destination that is about an hour away. Suggest visiting a relative or going to a diner in another town. The two of you could talk quietly then. Things would come up casually with no strain. It may sound strange, but it's what you have to do in order to satisfy your suffering parents. Now that you are becoming more and more involved with friends and other normal teenage pursuits, they are feeling left out of your life. It's best for everyone if you let them feel involved.

One of the favorite complaints teenagers have about parents embarrassing them is in the area of dress or physical appearance. Rob, 15, says,

My father wears an unbuttoned shirt with gold chains. He thinks he looks cool. . . .

Marissa, 13, says,

I was worried that my father was going to wear something really retarded, like those bermuda shorts, and embarrass the hell out of me when he came to pick me up from camp.

Karen, 14, says,

I hate when my mother wears shorts and a head-band. I mean, she tries to look like a teenager, but she's really making a fool of herself. I wish she'd dress normal.

Lets face it. You can't tell your parents how to dress. If you think about it, you don't like it when they tell *you* how to dress. The best way to handle the problem is to realize that you are separate from your parents. If people are looking at them, they are looking at them, and not you. People are not thinking of your parents in terms of you any more than they are thinking of you in terms of your parents. You and your parents are separate and responsible for your own appearances. Think about how you feel concerning your friends' parents' dress. You don't judge your friends by their parents' choice of clothing, do you? You probably just look and say, "Oh, that's inter-esting?" Or at worst you say, "I'm glad my parent doesn't dress that way," and you feel sorry for your friend.

See. There's no reason to be embarrassed at all.

Teenagers also get embarrassed by the physical appear-ance of their parents. Rodney, 16, says,

My mother has lots of facial hair, and sometimes I hear kids making comments about it. One time on parent-teacher night, I heard some kid say, here comes the lady with the mustache. I turned purple.

Sally, 17, says,

My mother is older than most parents. She had me late in life. I'm tired of all the kids asking, "Is *that* your mother."

Christine, 14, says,

My mother is so fat. I wish she would get in shape. I hate to be seen with her in the street.

So your mother is fat, your father limps, your mother has a mole on her face, your father drools at the mouth. *So what.* That's your parents, and they are not perfect. They did something right. They had you. You can thank them for that, and you can try to forgive them for not looking better than they do.

One way to cope with your embarrassment over your parents' faults is to think of all their good qualities. Make a list of all the things your parents have over other parents; things you think are special. Soon you'll be feeling proud of them, and the minor faults that embarrass you so much will seem unimportant.

Finally, don't feel guilty for being embarrassed by your parents. It's normal. Most teenagers go through a stage when they feel this way, but it passes. Soon you'll look back and wonder what in the world was so embarrassing. I'm ashamed to admit that I was embarrassed by my father's bald head and limp. He had a wooden leg from the knee down. He'd been run over by a train and survived. I used to hope he wouldn't come down the block while I was there with my friends, and then I'd feel so guilty for being ashamed of my own father that I couldn't sleep at night.

I think just knowing it's normal to be embarrassed and

realizing that no one else perceives things the way you do helps. Now I remember my friends thought I was crazy when I acted embarrassed of my father. In fact, they all liked him. He always stopped to say hello to them and he knew all their names. They liked him, and here I was being embarrassed.

Of course there will always be one ignoramus who will make fun of your parent, the way someone did of Rodney's mother for her facial hair. If anyone mocks your parent, I'm sure you'd be the first to tell that person off. That's when you know how you really feel about your parents. You're quick, very quick to defend them. Good for you!

In summary, whenever you are tempted to be embarrassed, whenever you think that people are looking at you, remember this: Most people are more concerned about a pimple on their nose than they are about your whole family history. They're really not thinking about you as much as you imagine they are.

Here are some reminders that will help you to cope with embarrassing situations that involve your parents.

1. Remember that parents do things in the heat of the moment. They have tempers, too.

2. Show your parents that you understand why they embarrassed you and then ask them if you could discuss it in private next time.

3. Remember that your parents are spontaneous. They don't always think about what they're going to do in terms of whether or not it will embarrass you. They're just living life.

4. Remember that parents like to have fun, too. They enjoy joking and laughing. They are bored with being straight.

5. Remember that you don't think anything of it when someone else's parents do something embarrassing, and

realize that people are not thinking anything of it when your parents do something that embarrasses you.

6. Remember to set aside private time for your parents.

7. Let your parents dress the way he or she wants to. No one is judging you by the way your parents dress. Realize that you are not responsible for your parents looks or behavior.

8. If you parent is physically imperfect, so what. If anyone insults your parents, he or she deserves to be told off.

9. Don't feel guilty about being embarrassed about your parents. It's normal, and as you mature you'll get over it.

10. Talk to your parents about times when their parents embarrassed them. This should help them to understand your feelings of embarrassment.

11. Make a list of things you admire about your parents. This will help you to forgive them for their imperfections. Instead of being embarrassed by them, you may be proud of them.

12. Refuse to get embarrassed. Picture people feeling sorry for you or thinking about their own lives.

Here is a chart that will help you to use some of the information gained in this chapter. Read the sample situation and then fill in your own experiences. Refer to it every time you feel yourself turning red.

SAMPLE SITUATION

Mother yelled at me in the store.

**WHY YOU FELT
EMBARRASSED**
People were staring.

**REASON NOT TO BE
EMBARRASSED**
They're probably thinking
about themselves.

**WHY YOU FELT
EMBARRASSED**

**REASON NOT TO BE
EMBARRASSED**

**WHY YOU FELT
EMBARRASSED**

**REASON NOT TO BE
EMBARRASSED**

**WHY YOU FELT
EMBARRASSED**

**REASON NOT TO BE
EMBARRASSED**

7

Hot Topics: Sex and Other Unmentionables

Sometimes we have a nice conversation, and the next minute we're having a furious argument. I don't know whether to talk to them or just be quiet and be safe.

Kristina, 15

Certain subjects seem to trigger explosions. You probably think it's your parents who blow up, but if you think about it, you probably contribute to the fireworks. In the back of your mind you may think you know what they're going to say, so the moment they utter a word you don't like, you start saying things like, "You just don't understand," or "I knew it . . ." before you've even heard them out.

– SEX –

One of the favorite explosive topics is sex. Many parents begin preaching a mile a minute whenever anything relating to sex comes up, and most teenagers either simply tune parents out or begin protesting.

First it would help if you could understand why most parents are so emotionally involved when it comes to you and sex. Your parents have obviously lived longer than you, and they have learned some basic truths about life. In short, they "know things," and they realize that you don't know these things. For example, when it comes to sex, your parents know that sex is a two-edged sword—you can be hurt by either side of it.

On the one hand, you can simply have sex. You can "leap into bed" with anyone just for the sheer fun of it. But they—as well as psychologists and psychiatrists who deal with emotionally disturbed people—know that this can lead to loss of self-respect. As one psychologist expresses it, when sex is too casual, you take your body and make it into "an object to be treated mechanically." But the body was not meant for mechanical treatment, but rather for intense, close mental-spiritual communion.[1]

But—and here's the other side of the two-edged sword—if you carefully choose the person with whom you go to bed and if you love that person and have close mental-spiritual communion with him or her, you have another problem that can emerge. You may become bonded to that person—so emotionally involved, that all of your creative energy is spent on that person. Your mind would become preoccupied with the relationship, when it should be free to deal with other growing up problems (choosing a career, learning to make decisions, etc). In addition, you may be unable to resist the force of "love," and you may make a wrong decision and marry that person. A sexual relationship at any age can be confusing because

[1]Rollo May, *The Courage to Create* (New York: Bantam Books, 1975), p. 10.

it's difficult to separate deep love from other feelings of closeness. But the older you are, the more you will understand your own emotions.

Since your parents have learned the truth about the two-edged sword of sex, naturally they want to protect you from being cut and even destroyed by that sword. They don't want you to lose respect for yourself by having casual sex, and they don't want you to become emotionally swept away either. In addition, many parents believe it is morally wrong to have sex outside of marriage. Your having sexual relationships may cut directly across their entire value system.

Finally, they fear that you will become pregnant. One mother says to her 15-year-old, Gloria,

> If you get pregnant, you can pack your bags and live in poverty with your boyfriend. Who will support two high-school students? Not me.

The only way to calm your parents down and to stop them from sermonizing about sex is to show them that you are well aware of what sex involves. Instead of becoming upset when they lecture you, let them talk. Listen carefully to what they have to say. See if their warnings involve any of the points mentioned above. Then think about it and see if you agree with them. If you do, let them know.

For example, if your mother is like Diane's mother:

> My mother kills me. She's always saying, "If you're doing things with boys, you'll be sorry. Boys will lose respect for you. You'll be sorry. I know you think this is a different age, but some things never change. . . ."

Why not ask some questions. "What never changes, Mom?" Let your mother talk about her feelings about casual sex. Then you can tell her that you agree and that you also feel that jumping into bed with lots of different partners is the worst thing you can do for your self-respect.

But what if you've already had a sexual relationship? Do you have to tell your mother, and are you being a phony if you don't? You have to decide whether or not you can confide in your mother about your sex life. But whether you have or haven't had sex, the important thing is, do you agree with her that casual sex is not the best thing? If so, there's no reason why you couldn't tell your mother that your ideas line up with hers. After all, your sexual experience may not have seemed casual to you. It's up to you if you want to explain that fact—but there's nothing dishonest in letting her know you take sex seriously.

What if you don't agree with your parents about sex. Suppose you think it is perfectly all right to have lots of different partners. Many males feel this way. It's the old "double standard." (Today many females also feel this way.) Then you can at least tell your parents that their ideas may be right and that they must know things because they have had more experience than you. Tell them outright that you are going to be doing a lot of thinking about what they said about sex. And mean it. An ignorant person thinks he or she knows everything already. That person has a closed mind. Such a mind is afraid of new ideas—it doesn't want to do the work of rethinking anything. It leads the way to limited pleasures and lots of hurt.

When you think about it, what harm is there in listening to your parents' ideas? No one can in the end force you to follow their ideas. When you realize this, maybe you can relax and let them have their say. The topic will cool off immediately. No matter how excited they are, your calmness will relax them.

Another explosive subject relating to sex is that of birth control. A 39-year-old mother of a 17-year-old girl says,

Genine asked me to get her birth control pills. I was shocked. She said, "I'm getting older now, and I want to be prepared in case I have sex." I was horrified. I brought up my girls to believe in virginity until married. How did she get those ideas, and then what gave her the nerve to ask me to help her to do something I always taught her was wrong?

Genine's mother is probably feeling like a failure as a mother. She tried to bring up her daughter to share her ideal—"a girl should be a virgin when she gets married." Obviously Genine is thinking in another direction. But Genine is being insensitive and thoughtless regarding her mother's feelings. It's one thing to have a mind of your own, to reject some of your parents' values, but it's quite another to ask them to be a party to what they consider to be a violation of their values. Genine should seek out her own birth control devices. There are hundreds of clinics and other places where birth control can be readily obtained today. In fact, most schools today have a counseling service (your guidance counselor can put you in touch with them) regarding birth control.

I'm not suggesting that Genine be "sneaky" and hide her intentions from her mother. If she wishes to have an open relationship with her mother, she could tell her mother that she isn't sure she agrees with the idea of waiting until you're married to have sex and that she was thinking about this a lot. She could even tell her mother that she intends to have sex before marriage. But to expect her mother to supply her with birth control so that she can do what her mother believes is wrong is a mistake. If Genine is mature enough to think logically about making a decision to have sex, and if she is wise enough to prepare herself by planning to use birth control, then she is perfectly capable of getting the birth control herself. In this case the topic will always be hot but not as hot as it would be if you add insult to injury and ask your parents to help you do what they don't believe you should be doing in the first place.

Sometimes the topic of sex is "hot," not because of your not wanting to discuss it but because of your parents' fear of the topic. Denise, 15, says,

When I ask my mother questions about sex, she gets that embarrassed look on her face, and that embarrasses me. She tells me she'll get me a book about it, but I want to know what *she* has to say.

Frankie, 16, says,

My father never in his life talked to me about the birds and the bees. I think I learned it all by myself. I think he's too embarrassed to talk about it. When I talk to him about girls, I just leave out the details, but sometimes I wish I didn't have to.

Many parents die of embarrassment when it comes to talking to their teenagers about sex, possibly because their own parents never discussed sex with them. These same parents probably even feel uncomfortable talking about it, with their close friends. Years ago sex was not a topic of public conversation. You can pick this up by watching old movies. Everything was implied. Nothing was spelled out as it is today.

How can you help your embarrassed parents talk about sex? The best thing to do is to bring out into the open that you know they hate to talk about sex because it embarrasses them. For example, Denise might say something like,

Mom, I know how hard it is for you to talk about sex with me. It's hard for me, too, but there are certain things I really want to know about, and I don't trust anyone else but you.

Mothers will feel a responsibility to answer their daughters' questions if put this way, because they wouldn't want their daughters to find answers in "the wrong" place. Also mothers would be flattered to know that their daughters have such confidence in them. Most mothers would find they would set aside their embarrassment and let their daughters ask the questions. After the first few minutes the conversation would run smoothly.

Frankie could open up the topic of sex with his father by saying something like,

> Dad, you know we never had a talk about the birds and the bees. I'm not a kid anymore, so I know what's going on, but I would like to know your ideas about certain things. Do you mind if I ask you a couple of questions. I mean, it's a little embarrassing, but you are my father, and...

It would take courage, but if Frankie did it, his father would have to respond.

If you are persistent, your "embarrassed" parent will answer your questions. A 41-year-old mother says,

> I'll never forget the time she asked me about oral sex. I mean, she didn't say it that way, she used a slang term. She was ten years old then, and I didn't want to answer, but there was no choice. I explained it as best I could. That woke me up to the fact that I'd better be ready for more questions as she grows up. When I thought about it, I was glad she had enough trust in me to ask *me*.

So if sex is a topic too hot for your parents to handle, and if it isn't too hot for you, then don't give up. Keep on asking. Eventually they'll put aside their embarrassment and talk to you, and you won't be sorry, because you'll have a closer relationship with your parents.

– HOMOSEXUALITY –

Perhaps the hottest topic relating to sex is that of homosexuality. Gary, 16, says,

My father is always giving me digs because I don't play football or do things that boys are supposed to do. He asks me why I don't have any girlfriends. How can I tell him I might be gay?

Instead of telling his father, Gary should speak to a counselor. Parents are too close to the situation to react calmly, I think. Sometimes a qualified stranger can give calm insight into the situation. Obviously Gary is not sure he's gay, he says "might be." He needs to understand himself better, and speaking to an objective person would help.

Homosexuality is not something to be taken lightly. It is also foolish to jump to the conclusion that you are homosexual just because you have had certain thoughts or even an experience. Psychologists say that it is normal for adolescents to go through such experiences and that many adolescents do have at least one homosexual experience, despite the fact that they are heterosexual.

If Gary were to speak with a psychologist, he could get his confusion straightened out. The psychologist could also help him to speak with his parents about his feelings.

If, on the other hand, Gary felt that he could trust his parents, if he sensed that they would back him up and give him support, he might tell them of his doubts. Some parents are very understanding, and instead of jumping down your throat, they will listen sympathetically. Such parents, if they cannot help you, will get you the professional help you need. If they can't cope with the problem you present to them, they themselves will get professional help.

If you are faced with questions about your sexuality, my advice to you is don't go it alone. If you can't talk to your parents, go to someone you can trust and/or talk to a psychologist. You deserve the opportunity to sort out your feelings.

– CAREERS –

Another hot topic, are you ready for this, is your future career. For some strange reason, many parents get worked up when their teenagers start talking about what they want to do with their future. Possibly they do this because they want to make sure you don't make the same mistake they did. They want you to have a better life. A 41-year-old father says,

> I didn't go to college, and I have to work like a dog for every dime I bring home. I'm making sure my son goes to college.

Can you picture what this father would say if his son started talking about becoming a construction worker?

Your parents mean well, but they sometimes forget that you have a mind and a personality of your own. You may be a creative person, someone who is gifted in the arts— writing, music, or painting. Your parents may be more practical and may want to push you into becoming a computer programmer or a business manager. You try to explain that you feel special, different, and they say, "You'll learn." But they may be wrong. Carl Jung, a well-known psychiatrist, points out that creative people are driven by an "inner law." Such people are compelled to pursue their own callings.[2]

Your parent may not understand this inner law, because he or she may be less creative. Intelligence has nothing to do with it. Your parent may be a genius, but be of a very practical nature. Very often, no one truly understands a creative person, because that person sees the world in a unique way. The very nature of creativity implies "originality" of "onliness" in effect, when you are crea-

[2]Carl G. Jung, *Memories, Dreams, Reflections, ed. Amelia Jaffe, trans. Richard and Clara Winston (New York: Random House, Vintage Books, 1961), pp. 356–357.*

tive, you must be ready to follow your own inner voice. If this is so, you will find some opposition. Evan, 17, says,

> I want to be a musician. I've written a few songs and they're being considered for publication. I play guitar and I plan to make a career out of music. My father keeps saying I'll end up on skid row with all the paupers or become a drug addict. He thinks all musicians are losers.

Evan's father pictures his son poor and on drugs. It isn't the music he opposes, it's what he perceives as the result of a career in music. Behind Evan's father's protest is his desire for his son to lead a safe, successful, happy life. Evan has to show his father that he is aware of the risks involved in pursuing a career in music. He could indicate that he is willing to go to college and major in music. This might make his father feel better, since most parents would like their children to have a college education and a college education does open up additional opportunities as a backup.

Other parents oppose their child because they don't believe he or she can actually fulfill the dream. Such parents think they know their teen but they perhaps underestimate their teen's determination and drive. This can be both frustrating and demoralizing.

> I told my mother I wanted to be a doctor and she laughed at me. "Are you kidding," she said. "Do you know how many years you'll have to go to school for that. And who do you think has the money to support you while you're being a lifetime student. Stop dreaming. Why don't you get a good job, and you'll probably marry a doctor." I could scream at her. I don't want to marry a doctor, I want to *be* one.

Stacey, 16

It's tough when your parent doesn't back you up in your dream. But take courage. If you hear an inner voice, a voice that Abraham Maslow, a well-known psychiatrist calls your "call in life," be true to it anyway. If you are not, you will be sorry for the rest of your life. Maslow says,

> Do not deny it out of weakness or for any other reason. He who belies his talents, the born painter who sells stockings instead, the intelligent man who lives a stupid life, the man who sees truth and keep his mouth shut . . . all these people perceive in a deep way that they have done wrong to themselves and they despise themselves for it.[3]

You'll never be happy until you fulfill that inner call. I took a roundabout route to mine. I always wanted to be an English teacher and a writer, but my parents didn't encourage me to go to college. In those days it was a luxury that very few people in my neighborhood could afford. I was told it might be a waste of time. I would get married and have babies anyway. Why bother with all that schooling. I became a secretary, and I hated it. I went back to school, but still listening to "practical" advice, I majored in retailing. I was going to be a buyer so I could make money. I hated retailing, and after wasting another year in a community college, I finally found the courage to do what I really wanted. I applied to a liberal arts college and was accepted under the conditions that I make up certain high-school academic subjects. To make a long story short, not only did I graduate from college, I went on and got a master's degree and a Ph.D. as well. I became an English teacher in high school and college, and a writer, too. If I had let others stop me from my dream, I know that right now I would be miserable—like the person described by Maslow—I would despise myself.

[3]Abraham Maslow, *Toward a Psychology of Being* (New York: D. Van Nostrand Company, 1968), p. 7.

Instead I'm happy and excited about life. Every day is an adventure, and I'm often asked the question, "Why are you so full of energy and joy?" The simple truth is, when you are doing what you are supposed to be doing with your life, you are happy. You're "in your place," like a piece in a puzzle. But when you're doing something that is not suited to your being, you're like a misfit piece—like a square peg jammed into a round hole. You never feel comfortable.

I'm not telling you to defy your parents, to ignore what they say. Instead listen to them but pursue your dream.

In order to create a peaceful atmosphere at home, you will have to explain to your parents how you feel. Talk to them about your interests and excitements. Let them know that you want to end up in a career that you love and not in a job that you dread going to on Monday mornings.

You should allow your parents to explain why your preferred career is not a good one and why the career they have in mind for you is better. Ask them to sit down with you and list the pros and cons of their choice, while you do the same for yours. Then you can both review the lists.

Some teenagers I know have ended up looking into the career their parents had in mind, and, much to their surprise, found it exciting. You may not change your mind, but at least you will show that you are open-minded and are willing to consider other possibilities. This will help to unfrustrate your parent who thinks you're not being realistic.

– DRUGS –

A very hot topic today with parents and teenagers is drugs. You may wonder, "Why would teenagers want to talk to parents about drugs?" Freddy, 16, says,

I'd like to tell my father that I get high because I don't think it's so wrong, but I'm afraid he'd blow up at me. Whenever I try to bring it up, he starts talking about how nobody did drugs in his day.

Freddy says he doesn't think getting high "is so wrong," but he's well aware of the fact that his father would certainly think it is. It's foolish for you to expect your parent to condone your doing drugs of any kind. The only time to let your parent in on the fact that you do drugs is when you are planning to stop doing them. Maybe Freddy, in his deeper self, wants to stop getting high, and for this reason he's tempted to tell his father. Unconsciously he wants to be stopped, so he toys with the idea of telling his father. Then he loses courage and gives himself a reason to not open up.

Jason, 17, did find the courage to tell his father, even though he thought his father would hit the ceiling.

I didn't have to admit that I was doing coke, but I decided to tell everything anyway. I had been taking money from the house and buying drugs, and my parents were asking a lot of questions. I was always high on coke, and my mother was looking suspiciously at me a lot. Finally, one day I couldn't stand the pressure and I blurted out the whole thing to my dad. Now my father is not the calm type. I expected him to go crazy. Instead he looked very worried and stayed quiet for a while. Then he looked up and said, "We're going to have to get help for you." Later we all sat down, and I agreed to see a counselor. I ended up liking the guy, and now I'm doing better in school and no more drugs.

Your parents may surprise you if you dare to confide in them. Most parents will be so relieved that you are coming to them for help that they will put aside their impulse to punish you and instead use the energy to help you.

Think of it this way. If it's a hot topic, it is dangerous to handle. It's scary. It take a courageous person, someone with nerve to open up such a topic. Take the challenge and give it a shot. What's the worst thing that can happen? Back to square one. No progress. Mad fighting. But what's the best thing that could happen? You might get help, and you might feel much better about your life. In either case, you'll feel better about yourself because you had the courage to try to try to talk to your parents.

If your parents do go wild when you tell them that you have been doing drugs, understand that they are probably feeling a lot of guilt. They blame themselves for not keeping a closer watch on you and for failing in other ways as parents. After they calm down, you could reassure them by telling them that it's not their fault you got involved in drugs. It was your decision, a bad one—a mistake that with their help you intend to correct now. They'll feel comforted by such words, even if they don't admit it. It will calm them down inside.

– DIVORCE –

Other hot topics involve divorced parents. If your mother and father are divorced, chances are you can't talk about the absent parent to the other parent without hearing a whole story on how "bad" that parent is. It may hurt you to hear negative things said about your own mother or father, and you may find yourself defending that parent at the expense of an argument. Lincoln, 16, says,

One thing I can't talk to my mother about is my father. She has a negative attitude any time his name is brought up. If I say anything good about him, she comes out with a list of his faults. I love my father, and I find myself talking about him, but I have to check myself around my mother.

Most parents know that it is unproductive to speak negatively to a child about his or her absent parent no matter how imperfect that parent is. Yet many parents do it. Why? They are so angry with that person for many personal reasons that they let emotion take control. They find it impossible to say a good word about that person, even though they know it is destructive to say negative things to their children about their own parent.

Your parents may have hurt each other a lot before and during the divorce. They may be holding grudges against each other. If you find yourself in a situation where your mother is bad-mouthing your father (or your father is bad-mouthing your mother), you might say,

> I know how angry you are with . . . Daddy but he's still my father. It really hurts me when you say those things. It won't do me any good to hate him, too, will it? Now that he's out of your life, can't you bury the past, or at least forget him because he's my father.

This might cause your parent to think rationally and to cool it. If that doesn't work, you can ask a relative to speak to your parent. You can ask that relative not to mention that you asked him or her to talk to your parent, but rather to approach the subject casually. If your parent hears it from another party, he or she may think about it and eventually change his or her behavior.

Finally, many parents have trouble dealing with the cry "Why can't I go and live with my father," or "I'd rather be living with Mommy." There are many reasons for parents' getting upset when you ask to go and live with the other parent. First, your parent may think of him or herself as a personal failure. Here I am, they may think, doing all the work, trying to make a good life for us, and it's still not enough. After all my effort, he (she) still wants to go and live with ———.

Next, your parent may see your wish to go to your other parent as rejection. Parents should be mature, you might argue. They should be above that feeling. But being human, they are not. Your parents may think that your expressed desire to live with the other parent is like saying, "I don't like you as much as ————. I chose Dad (or Mom, whatever the case may be) over you."

Finally, your parent may simply not want to even think of your leaving and going to live with the other parent because he or she loves you so much and it would hurt him or her too deeply to not have you around every day. Granted, you and your parent may not get along all the time, but your parent has a deep love for you, and the thought of your not being around fills him or her with dread. Your absence would leave a very empty space, and your mentioning that you would like to leave and go live with the other parent fills your parent with sadness.

All of these reasons and lots of others that are deeply psychological combine to make your parent become very defensive, protective, and even angry when you suggest that you want to live with the other parent. The only intelligent way to approach the topic is not in the heat of anger but rather in a cool, logical discussion. David, 14, says,

My mother and father got divorced when I was thirteen. I used to be very close to my father, and it really hurt me. When I got to be fourteen, I couldn't stand it anymore and I came out and asked if I could go and live with my father. At first she said "No way." But then I explained myself. I told her that I love her very much but I needed to be with my father—there were things I couldn't talk about with her. She calmed down and said she would talk it over with my father.

David may or may not have ended up living with his father. The point is, he got a hearing. By appealing to his mother's logic (she must know that most boys find it easier to talk to their fathers than to their mothers about certain topics), he took the issue away from the area of his mother's emotions. Instead of feeling like a failure, instead of feeling rejected, and instead of allowing herself to envision her own loneliness, she thought about David's needs and was willing to consider the possibility of letting him go to live with his father.

Often it is not possible to change your living arrangement because one parent isn't capable of taking care of you (for whatever reason). If you know this, there is no sense in continually saying that you want to live with the other parent. It can only be frustrating to the parent you're living with, and it will cause an explosive argument. In short, if you know full well that there's no possibility of your going to live with the other parent, keep your wishful thinking to yourself. It isn't wrong to wish, but unless your goal is to do battle with your parent, it pays to use self-control.

In summary, if you do think there's hope for a change of living arrangements, the way to approach it is with love and logic. First let your parent know how much you love and appreciate him or her and then give your honest reasons for wanting to go and live with the other parent.

Hot topics are the biggest cause of frustration between parents and teenagers. You have a choice. You can either let things go along the way they are now, or you can take action and change things. Remember, "It isn't them. It's you. You could change it all."[4] Don't wait for your parents to change. You change them.

Here are some reminders.

1. Your parents have lived a long time and they know things. Listen to what they have to say. Ask them questions and consider their point of view.

2. Show your parents that you are well aware of the dangers they are warning you about.

[4]Ari Kiev, M.D., *Riding through the Downers, Hassles, Snags and Funks* (New York: E. P. Dutton & Company, 1980), p. 19.

3. Agree with your parents whenever you can honestly do so. Let them know you do with enthusiasm.

4. If you disagree with your parents, let them know that you are thinking about what they have to say.

5. Don't expect your parents to help you to do something they believe is wrong.

6. Help your parents to talk about embarrassing topics by letting them know you understand how they feel and then expressing a need for advice.

7. Certain topics are too hot for your parents to handle. Speak to a trained counselor.

8. Help your parents to understand that you have a dream that is very special to you, but listen to their point of view.

9. Take a chance and confide in your parents. They may surprise you by being understanding and coming to your aid.

10. If your parent is speaking ill of your other parent, tell that parent how much talk hurts your feelings.

Here is a chart that will help you to use some of the information gained in this chapter. Read the sample situation and then fill in the chart with your own experiences.

SAMPLE SITUATION

My father started warning me about having sex with boys.

WRONG REACTION	RESULT
"I hate when you start talking about that. What do you think I am anyway?"	A heated argument and a long lecture.

NEW REACTION
Listen to him and ask, "What do you mean? Why do you say that?" Agree with him and say, "I'll keep in mind what you said."

RESULT
Father calmed down and said, "I'm glad to see I'm raising a daughter with a good head on her shoulders."

TYPICAL SITUATION

WRONG REACTION

RESULT

NEW REACTION

RESULT

TYPICAL SITUATION

WRONG REACTION

RESULT

NEW REACTION

RESULT

TYPICAL SITUATION

WRONG REACTION   **RESULT**

NEW REACTION   **RESULT**

8

It's Just Not Fair!

The most horrible incident in my life was when my mother read by diary....

Denise, 16

My parents promised I could go to the party, then for no reason, they changed their minds.

Tama, 14

I'm the middle child, and I always get the worst end of the deal....

Frankie, 16

When it comes to being unfair, parents are guilty in the first degree, and they admit it.

Sometimes I worry so much about her that I go through her things to see if she's doing drugs or anything. I know I shouldn't but...

41-year-old mother

I know I should keep my word, but things happen and I just can't. I feel really bad....

42-year-old father

I know it's wrong to compare, but I can't help it. I catch myself doing it a lot.

39-year-old mother

There are probably hundreds of "unfair" situations that arise between you and your parents. They may invade your privacy, go back on their word, favor your brothers and sisters over you, make unfair demands, and provoke you to a rage and then punish you for talking back. Sometimes you think you hate them, and then you feel guilty because you know they love you. Is there no end to this unhappy state of affairs?

Yes. There is a solution, but in order to find it, you'll have to put your ego aside and, again, think from your parents' point of view.

Parents are unfair for hundreds of reasons. It all depends on the particular situation. For example, the mother who read her daughter's diary admits that she was worried that her daughter was "doing things" and that she should know about them before it's too late. The parents who promised that Tama could go to the party and then changed their minds admit that after they had thought about it, they realized it wasn't wise to let their daughter hang out with that crowd because there were a lot of drugs going on (later they did some checking about that group of teenagers). And Frankie's mother and father admitted to me that they do tend to pay more attention to their oldest and youngest child and that they know how hard it is for Frankie, but...

It's clear that parents aren't unfair just to be mean. In fact, they feel really bad about being unfair. They may not always admit this to you, but there's a reason for this. It's probably because you accuse them of being unfair. You *attack* them. For example, in the case of Tama and the party, she may say to her parents,

> You promised! See what I mean! You're just never fair. I'll never trust you again. You lied to me...

Causing her parents to respond,

> We'll do whatever we think is right for you, young lady. We're entitled to make decisions, and we realized we made a mistake. You'll just have to live with it, and watch your mouth, or you'll be punished....

But what if Tama had said something like

> Mom, Dad, I think I understand why you changed your minds. You probably said I could go before you really had a chance to think about it, but then when you had time, you thought that there may be some people there you don't want me to hang around with. I appreciate your worries, but really, there's no reason to be concerned. ———'s mother will be there. Let me call her and put you on the phone with her. And by the way, if any of the wrong crowd comes around, I'll stay away from them or just leave. Give me a chance to prove myself.

This approach sympathizes with your parents' position. It is quite the opposite of sympathizing with your own position, which leads to attacking your parents and accusing them of being this and that and telling them you'll never trust them again. The latter approach makes you feel good for the moment. You get it off your chest and tell them off. But what good does it do your cause? You're still stuck with the unfair decision. Isn't it better to put your ego to the side, use self-control and a little psychology, and see things from your parents' point of view? Almost always this will lead to a compromise solution. Very few parents would be able to resist such an approach. What's more, it would help them feel that you are reliable, growing up, and able to be trusted a bit more.

What if Denise, whose mother read her diary, screamed at her mother, "I'll never trust you again." Her mother would probably defend herself and say, "Well, you should keep it locked up." Instead if Denise said,

> I feel very betrayed. I always trusted you, and I never dreamed you would invade my privacy. Now I feel as if I can't keep a diary. Why did you do it, Mom?

Then her mother would probably admit that she did it because she was worried that Denise was doing things that would get her into trouble, and she would be likely to admit she was wrong to do it. Denise could then say something like

> I know how hard it must be to see me grow up. You must have all kinds of fears going through your mind, about sex or doing drugs or cutting school. I guess you figured my diary would tell it all. But Mom, you'll have to trust me. You taught me to trust and to respect people's privacy, and I believe you're right. I know you did it because you had my best interest at heart, but I need you to promise that you'll never do it again. I want to trust you again, Mom, but I'm hurt.

Notice that Denise would be using the method of sympathizing with her parents' point of view. In addition, however, she would be using another method called "giving one a fine reputation to live up to" or "appealing to noble motives." By her reminding her mother that she (her mother) had taught her (Denise) to respect people's privacy, her mother would be compelled to follow her own good teaching example. Denise should never say something like "You taught me to respect people's privacy, and then you invade mine. You're a hypocrite." By doing this, she would be forcing her mother to defend herself, and in addition, she would be giving her mother a bad reputation to live up to. Denise's mother may think to herself, "Well, I did it once. I might as well do it again." By appealing to a higher motive, Denise can help her mother to live up to her own value: respect for people's privacy.

I know it would be very, very difficult for Denise to use the kind of self-control involved to say these things, so there is an alternative. She could tell her mother off first, and then have this conversation at a later date. That's okay, too. But the point is, she should have the conversation.

Whenever you're about to react to an unfair situation, ask yourself, "What is my goal," and then act. If your goal is to make the situation fair, you'll find yourself checking your words and changing them to other well-thought-out words.

Frankie, the left-out middle child, could say to his parents, "You don't love me. I can tell because I don't get the same treatment you give ———" With that accusation, Frankie's parents would probably defend themselves and say, "Of course we love you as much, it's just that..."

But what if Frankie said something like this:

You know, it seems to me as if I have no special place in this family. Joe is older, and he gets more privileges than I do. Carey is the youngest and she gets away with everything, and you're always making a big fuss over how cute she is. I feel as if I'm nothing around here. I have an idea; why don't you take one day a week and make a big deal out of me.

You may be thinking, "That's ridiculous. Nobody would say that to their parents." Right. Nobody usual. But you would because you're unusual and you're willing to take a chance. Now listen to the hidden psychology. You're not really expecting your parents to take one day a week and make a big fuss over you (although that wouldn't be a bad idea at that), but by making that speech and that request, you'd be giving your parents a clear message in a form they could accept. You want special attention, too. You're feeling neglected. Your parents would examine their behavior and feel immediately justified in changing their attitude toward you. In fact, they'll be glad that you were courageous enough to bring it to their attention, and they'll be happy that you showed them before it was too late and they did damage to your self-image.

Notice that Frankie did not use the method of sympathizing with his parents, but on the other hand, he certainly did not attack them. Instead he took a middle road and adopted what I call the "humble sufferer" stance. He simply expressed his position in nonaccusatory terms. Then he came up with a solution, what I call the "positive suggestion" method. When something is wrong, it's not always enough to point out what's wrong. It's usually necessary for you to suggest a way to make things better. Your parents really do need all the help they can get in making your life better, and the best help they can get, if you think about it, is a suggestion directly from you— the one whose life should be better.

It's not only unfair to be compared unfavorably to brothers, sisters, or friends, it's painful. I can still recall my own mother saying, "Barbara had no trouble learning this. What's wrong with you?..." I remember thinking, "I wish I were smarter. I wish I could learn as fast as Barbara." And then I felt inferior. But in my case, it worked for my best interest. I got so angry that I tried twice as hard as Barbara, and I ended up doing very well.

No matter how you react, however, it's difficult not to hold unfair comparisons against brothers or sisters.

Every time my mother compares me to my sister, I hate my sister. "Your sister is always so sweet. *She* never gives me a smart answer. Your sister never argues with me . . . and so on and so forth.

Dana, 16

Instead of hating her sister, what if Dana confronted her mother with the facts. She might say,

Mom, no matter how hard I try, I can never be Rhona. I know Rhona is much sweeter than I am and that you and Rhona get along better than you and I do, but every time you tell me about that, I start resenting Rhona. Can't you just treat me as an individual. Then maybe I can work on being a better daughter to you.

In addition, Dana might ask her mother if her parents ever compared her to her older sister or to friends. She might ask if this made her feel bad.

By using the above method, Dana would be helping her mother to realize that she (Dana) is an individual and that it is unfair to expect her to mold her behavior after anyone else's. She would also be pointing out that her mother is causing unnecessary anger between sisters. Most parents strive very hard to keep sibling rivalry at a minimum. They know that there's enough natural sibling rivalry among brothers and sisters without their provoking more and unhealthy rivalry. No parents are happy when their own children hate each other. They are in fact happy when their children love and defend one another.

In addition, by asking her mother if her own parents ever compared her, Dana would be using the method of empathy. She would be forcing her mother to put herself in Dana's place and remember how it feels to be compared. This will help her mother see how angry and frustrated one can become when one is constantly "compared."

Comparing is a bad habit, one that your parents should

be encouraged to break. Whether they compare you to siblings or friends, it's your responsibility to alert them to the fact that they are doing it and that it makes you unhappy. Tyrone, 15 says,

> The next time my parents compare me to my friends and say, "Why are you so fat. None of your friends are overweight," I'm going to tell them, the more you compare me to them, the more I eat because I get depressed when I think of myself being the only fat one.

If Tyrone said that and then added, "Help me to go on a diet, but please don't compare me to others," I'm sure his parents would get the message.

– "DON'T I HAVE A RIGHT TO STICK UP FOR MYSELF?" –

Did your parents ever insult or provoke you to the point where you got so angry you couldn't take it any more? Before you could stop yourself, you said something very fresh and a second later received a slap in the face or a major punishment. That doesn't seem fair, does it? Monique, 15, says,

> My mother gets real snotty sometimes. I mean, if we're having an argument, she starts calling me all kinds of things, and I'm just supposed to sit there and take it. I said, "I hate you," and then called her a few names, too. She jumped up and slapped me so hard I thought my face would fall off. How is it that she can say anything she wants, and when I say anything I get hit?

It's a tough situation. Even the Bible tells parents not to provoke their children, but parents seem to have skipped over that passage. The only one they seem to remember clearly is the one about honoring your father and your mother. But parents don't really want to provoke you. As mentioned before, they just become so frustrated that they start calling you the names they fear you will be if they don't keep after you. For example, if your father calls you a lazy, stupid bum, what he's saying is, I'm afraid you will be . . . and so on. Naturally you hear these words and become enraged. You want to defend yourself or strike back.

But the next time your parent starts attacking you verbally, instead of striking back with words, say something like

> You're calling me lots of names now, and I'm about to explode. Yet if I do, I'll get punished. It isn't fair that I have to sit here and take it. I know I have to because if I don't I'll be punished. Can't we talk later when things calm down. I don't like to make you so angry either.

If this doesn't work, try,

> I know what you mean. I am lazy and stupid (or whatever you are being called). I guess there's no hope for me. No matter how many times you tell me, I always do the same stupid thing. I don't know why you even bother to try to help me. You must be so ashamed to have a son/daughter like me.

You'll have to be a good actor/actress for the second one, but if you are and you make it sound as if you mean it (act depressed and disgusted with yourself), your parent will probably reverse his or her position and start saying, "Don't call yourself names. You're only human. You're not lazy and stupid, you're just going through a stage. It will pass." This latter approach is called "reverse psychology." Instead of defending yourself, you attack yourself. It's difficult for two people to argue on the same side of an issue, just the way two fighters don't fight on the same side of the ring. If you defend yourself, your parent continues to take the opposite side of the ring and attack you, but if you attack yourself, watch your parent go on the other side of the ring and start defending you. But remember, you have to really get into it and seem dejected and disgusted with yourself for it to work.

Some people would say it's not fair to use such psychology on your parent. I say it is, because the end result justifies it. In the end, your parent will realize that he or she does not in fact think you are a no-account loser or whatever else he or she is calling you, and your parent will realize that he or she in fact thinks the world of you.

– "I CAN'T TELL ON MY OWN BROTHER!" –

Some parents put their children in the unfair position of expecting them to "tell" on each other. Here's what happened to Gene, 17.

My father and brother were arguing about something my brother was supposed to have done wrong, and my father asked me about it. I covered for him, but later my father found out the truth and blamed me for lying. I was grounded for two weeks. What was I supposed to do, tell on my own brother?

Gene did the right thing, but he paid for it. Most parents know that siblings are supposed to be loyal to one another, and they don't even request that they play detective against one another. Some parents, however, think that your loyalty is to them first and foremost. If your parents are this way, you might say something like

I know you have his best interest in mind and you think that by my not telling you what he did, I hurt him. But since I'm his brother, if I tell on him, he won't trust me and he'll hide what he does from me. We'll end up living in the same house like strangers or enemies. Please don't put me in the position where I have to either betray my own brother or lie to you. It's just not fair to me, and if you think about it, I'll bet you see what I mean.

In using this approach, you would be practicing the method of sympathizing. Then you would be using the method of indirect education—you'd be teaching your parents a truth, without making a big deal out of the fact that you (the teenager) are teaching them (the adults) something. Then you'd be using the method of "appeal to higher motives" (when you ask them to please not put you in that position and when you expect them to see what you mean if they think about it). The important thing to remember here is attitude. If you say the words in an angry, menacing fashion, of course your parents will pick up on that and ignore the words and continue to fight with you. You have to be calm and act like a diplomat. If you have to, wait until you cool off before you start talking to them.

– "WHY DO I HAVE TO JUMP WHEN THEY CALL?" –

Teenagers complain that their parents sometimes act like tyrants.

I could be sitting down watching my favorite television show, and just when the best part comes on, my mother yells, "Jodi," and if I don't answer, she comes in and starts demanding that I do something immediately.

Jodi, 14

I'm on the phone with my friend, and my father yells, get off the phone this minute and do the dishes. I try to tell him I'll do them later, but he keeps insisting until my conversation is ruined.

Robin, 15

I want to watch what I want to watch on television, but my mother says, It's my TV and my house. I say what we watch. All my friends have their own TVs but she won't get me my own because she's afraid I'll waste too much time with it.

Carmine, 16

In each of the above cases, the principle of "compromise" would work. Jodi could answer immediately and say, "Please, just two minutes until this part is over," then she could go in and see what her mother wants. She could then ask if she could wait until the commercial to do what is being asked and then *do it* when the commercial comes on. If she keeps her word and does it, her mother will be able to trust her for future times and will allow her the time she asks for. If, on the other hand, she is like some teenagers I know and she promises to do it during the commercial but then doesn't, naturally her mother will demand that she do it *now*.

Robin is probably guilty of not having done the dishes when she should have done them. If she wants peace on the telephone, she should make sure her responsibilities are out of the way before she gets on the phone. To buy time, however, she might say, "Dad, I know I should have done the dishes before I got on the phone. Next time I will. Could you give me exactly five minutes, and if I'm still not off, you can come in here and make me get off the phone." Her father might go for that, especially since she would be admitting that she should have taken care of the dishes first.

Carmine could ask his mother to make a deal with him. He could request that he be allowed to pick three television shows that he likes and be allowed to watch those shows, undisturbed. Asking for three shows a week isn't asking too much, and I think most parents would agree to that. The rest of the time Carmine could take his chances and watch what his family is watching or spend his time on more creative pursuits. He may not realize it, but his mother is doing him a favor by giving him a hard time with the television. He and everyone else would be a lot better off doing things than watching things.

Some parents unfairly demand that you work for them for free, like baby-sit for example. Trina, 14, says,

> My mother and father expect me to baby-sit whenever they feel like going out. In the meantime all my friends are out having fun. I don't even get paid to do it. What do they think I am, a slave?

Here again a compromise could be worked out. Trina could explain to her parents that all of her friends do baby-sitting jobs and that they are saving lots of money in the bank for the future. Trina might say something like

> I know it's convenient for you and Dad to have me baby-sit, and it does seem foolish for you to have to hire a sitter when I am right here. But I do have a life, too, and I could be baby-sitting outside and getting paid. Can't we work out a fair deal where I do a certain amount of baby-sitting for you as part of my responsibility of being a member of this family and the rest I either get paid for or don't *have* to do?

If Trina expresses herself this way, chances are her parents will realize that they have been "using" her unfairly and they will likely want to compromise. If, on the other hand, Trina says, "I'm not your built-in baby-sitter. No way am I going to sit for that brat," her parents will take the opposite extreme and say, "As long as you live in this house, you'll do as we say, young lady," and Trina will be sitting and hating it—for free.

– "WHY DO YOU ALWAYS SAY, 'ASK YOUR FATHER'?" –

Jeanie, 15, says,

> One thing I can't stand is when I ask my mother if I can go someplace and she says, "Ask your father." I know she's just copping out because she knows he will say no, or by the time I ask my father, it may be too late to go where I wanted to go because the girls already left for the amusement park or wherever I asked to go to. That makes me so mad I could scream.

Jeanie is right to be angry. It isn't fair when parents avoid dealing with an issue. They often do this because they don't want to be responsible for making a decision. They fall into the trap of what is called "passing the buck." How can you make the "buck stop here?" How can you get your parent to make a decision when it is needed on the spot? Jeanie's best bet would be to make her mother aware of her frustration but to do it in a noninsulating, calm way. Perhaps she could say something like

> Mom, most of the time when I want to do something, you tell me I have to wait for Dad. Do you think you could have one long talk with Dad so that you two could get your rules straight. It's really hard for me to keep waiting forever whenever I want to do something.

By asking her mother to have "one long talk" with Dad, Jeanie would be indirectly pointing out that her mother should get to the point where she and her father have enough of a joint philosophy on what is and what is not out of bounds that the world does not have to stop every time a decision has to be made. Of course Jeanie could have said something like

> What's wrong with you anyway. Don't you have a mind of your own?

But this approach would serve to reinforce her mother's behavior. Her mother might defend herself and say something like,

> Well, don't think you're going to get me to let you do things that your father doesn't agree on....

It's much better to point out the parents' fault indirectly. Most parents would at least give it some thought if their teenager were sensitive enough to avoid attacking while making a complaint.

In all fairness, I must tell you what the parents think is not fair. One mother, 39, says,

> Not fair? I'll tell you what's not fair. It's not fair that I have to spend my time trying to keep my daughter from messing up her life and then getting insulted by her for doing it. There's no reward. I want to have fun, go out, party, and be a person but no. I have to stay home and wait for her to get home. It's not fair that no one told me what it would be like to have a teenager, and it's not fair that now that I have one, I'm trapped. If I don't do my job and discipline her, she may turn out to be a loser and then I'll be sorry and also she'll never forgive me. If I do my job and stay on her back, she'll give me a hard time every step of the way, and I'll get old and ugly in the process. You talk about not fair. That's what's not fair.

Well, it may not be fair at the moment, but if you take the long view of life, there is fairness. But nothing is simple. With every pleasure there is some pain. With every high there is a low. With every privilege there is a responsibility. Parents have children and they are proud of the children, but they have to pay the price of raising them. Children grow up and become teenagers and start having the freedom of adults, but they have to pay the price of earning that freedom. Life deals us a hand of cards, and we have to make the best of that hand. It may not always seem fair, but if we work hard and use our heads, we can make it more fair in the long run. Life, like a big jigsaw puzzle, when put together, fits—is fair—in the long run. But you have to keep working on that puzzle to put it together, or you'll never have the pleasure of seeing the end result.

If you think your parents are being unfair to you in many ways, why not think about how you may be doing unfair things to them. Ask them to compile a list of things you do to them that they see as unfair. Then draw up your own list of things you feel they do that are unfair and exchange lists. Then try compromising with each other by trading off one unfair thing for another. You don't do this, if they won't do that.

In review, if your parents are unfair to you, remember,

1. See things from your parents' point of view. Analyze what made them do the unfair thing.

2. Express sympathy for their doing what they did, feeling what they feel.

3. Offer a compromise solution to the unfair situation.

4. Don't be too lazy to invest the time needed to make things fair.

5. Ask your parents questions about how their parents treated them. Help them to remember how unfair treatment feels.

6. Agree with your parents when they are verbally abusing you. They'll start defending you.

7. Learn to use the method of "indirect education."

8. Appeal to your parents' "higher motives."

9. Remember: In the long run, life can be fair—but you have to keep working to make it that way.

Here are some Nevers when dealing with unfair treatment.

1. Never attack your parents verbally (You're not fair. . . .)

2. Never put yourself in a position of vulnerability. Fulfill your responsibilities first, then have your fun.

3. Never forget that your parents think it's not fair, too.

Here is a chart that will help you to use some of the information gained in this chapter. Read the sample situation and then fill in the chart with your own experiences. It's up to you to figure out the new reaction every time you make a mistake. This way you'll be mentally prepared when the next opportunity arises.

SAMPLE SITUATION

My mother said, "Why can't you be like your sister?"

WRONG REACTION
"The hell with her. I'm me."

RESULT
My mother kept talking about my sister's doing things better than I do them.

NEW REACTION
"I can't be like ———. I'm different. But I'll try to do my best."

RESULT
"I'm sorry. I really shouldn't compare you two. It's not fair. Please remind me every time I do it."

TYPICAL SITUATION

WRONG REACTION   **RESULT**

NEW REACTION   **RESULT**

TYPICAL SITUATION

WRONG REACTION   **RESULT**

NEW REACTION   **RESULT**

TYPICAL SITUATION

WRONG REACTION   **RESULT**

NEW REACTION   **RESULT**

- - - - - - - - - - - - - -

9

Problem Parents or They Need Therapy

My mother is very nervous. If she's in the wrong mood, she'll take a swing at me. She's always saying I'm sorry I ever had kids.

Jessica, 17

When he's not drunk, he's stoned.

Gary, 15

My father tries to get fresh with me—then when I tell my mother, he denies it.

Corina, 14

Up until now we've been discussing normal parents who pose ordinary problems to their teenagers. But what do you do if your parent is out of control in some ways and may even need therapy?

If you remember that anyone can have children (that is to say, the government doesn't require people to take a test to see if they are mentally competent), it shouldn't surprise you that many parents have deep psychological problems. Don't panic, though. Later, I will show you that some of the most successful, and creative people have come from homes where one or both parents were deeply disturbed.

Problem parents range from those who are simply neurotic (having a disorder of the mind, filled with anxiety and fear, guilt, etc.) to those who are more seriously disturbed (those who physically or sexually abuse their children). A neurotic parent is basically nervous or jumpy. He or she is likely to blow things way out of proportion and be extremely inconsistent in his or her reaction to situations. Neurotic parents often overreact to things and often forcefully blame their children for things that they themselves feel guilty about. This kind of blame is called "projection"—the parent projects—throws out a picture of his or her own guilt as if it were being cast out by a projector—onto the teen. The parent sincerely believes that the teen is guilty of the behavior being projected. For example, a father who considers himself to be a failure because he chose the wrong profession and married the wrong woman may continually tell his son, "You're going to be a bum." In reality, the father thinks of himself as a bum. A mother who used to be a "lady of easy virtue" may call her daughter a whore. In reality, she is projecting her own guilt regarding her past behavior onto her daughter.

Neurotic parents are often filled with guilt and anxiety because of the way their own parents raised them. They may have had severely strict parents or parents who constantly criticized them, filling them with fear and inferiority complexes. Such parents may never have been able to get help to straighten out the problems caused by such an upbringing and may now be passing on their own insecurities to their children. Such parents may be afraid to take chances, and they may have something negative to say about any new venture. Teens interpret this as unloving behavior, but in reality it is a neurotic parent's way of protecting his or her child from what he or she sees as potential danger.

Neurotic parents suffer greatly. They sense that they are not being good parents, and they feel tremendous guilt whenever they do something to hurt their teen. They often apologize profusely and try to make up their misdeeds with excessive gifts or loving. Then a few minutes, hours, days, or weeks later, they do something hurtful again. They don't want to, but they can't control themselves. They need help. If your parent is neurotic, he or she is suffering more than you could ever imagine. That parent loves you but cannot find the power to give you the kind of love that will make you a happy, secure person.

Barbara, 16, has trouble with her neurotic mother:

> My mother keeps the house like a pigsty. I do all the cleaning and cooking. I have to pick up after her and everyone else. If I forget to clean the stove or something, she will come searching for me and screaming at the top of her lungs calling me a lazy good-for-nothing slob. She says when I get married, my husband will leave me. My father left when I was five years old. Maybe that's why she says it.

Barbara is on the right track. Karen Horney, a well-known psychologist, says that people who are unhappy with the way their own lives have turned out and who are disgusted with their own behavior often tend to shift the blame from themselves to others.[1] This is a case of what is called "projection." Since Barbara is not a psychologist, nor should she try to be one, she cannot hope to cure her mother of her problem. She can, however, make the situation either a little better or a little worse. The worst

[1]Karen Horney, M.D., *Neurosis and Human Growth* (New York: W. W. Norton & Company, 1950), pp. 15–17, 155–156.

thing Barbara could do would be to defend herself and say something like

> I'm not a slob. What about you. You're supposed to be the mother around here. Why do I have to do all the work.

Her mother would feel twice as guilty and defend herself and attack more viciously. What Barbara must do is relieve her mother of guilt by making her feel as if she's not such a failure as a mother. She might try,

> Mom. I love you so much. I wish I were more considerate of you. You try so hard to make a good life for us. I know it isn't easy for you. I'll try to do better, Mom.

Then she should give her mother a big hug.

I agree with you if you're thinking that this is impossible. After all, you're a teenager with a lot of teenage problems as it is. How are you going to be expected to use that kind of self-control. In addition, you probably resent the fact that you are stuck with a neurotic parent. I don't blame you for wanting to argue and fight back. It's perfectly normal. The only thing wrong with that is it will cause more and more fighting and more and more unhappiness. The ideal thing would be to get your parent to see a psychologist. I will discuss how later.

Some parents are well aware of the fact that they can't cope with raising children. They have enough trouble coping with living. They say things like Jennifer's mother says:

> "I'm counting the days until you get old enough to go out on your own." I hear that day and night. Or else she'll say, "I'm going to put you in a foster home or a shelter. You'd better not give me a hard time...."

A parent who says things like this is not necessarily neurotic but rather may be feeling very frustrated because he or she is having a hard time doing the job of parenting. But if your parent constantly says such things (every day or more), then your parent is a bit neurotic. It doesn't mean your parent doesn't love you. It means that your parent is admitting that he or she can't cope with being a parent and that your parent realizes that he or she can't just quit being a parent. There's no such thing as walking away from it. She's stuck. Once they have a child, parents have no choice but to raise you or give you away, and having chosen to raise you, their back is against the wall.

It hurts deeply to hear parents say they don't want you. It feels as if you are unloved and worthless. In reality, though, it has nothing to do with *you* in particular. It has only to do with the fact that your parents cannot cope with the frustrations and responsibilities of being parents and they are scared, guilty, and angry. They do love you, but right now they're taking out their frustration on you.

When a parent says something like "I wish I never had you," or "I can't wait until you leave," the most natural response is, "I didn't ask to be born. I wish I never were," or "I can't wait until I leave, too. I hate it here." Such talk will only cause more fighting. If you could use self-control and say something comforting to your parent, you might be surprised at the results. Something like

It must be very hard trying to raise teenagers today. I know I do ask for a lot, and I give you plenty of trouble. It seems as if you spend most of your time doing things for me. I wish I would grow up faster than I am, so I wouldn't be such a burden to you. Sometimes I hate being a teenager myself.

If you could say that with a sincere attitude, your parent would probably soften and keep the ugly talk to a minimum. If you think about why your parents say the ugly things (their own frustrations), it won't be so hard for you to comfort them. In the end you'll be the better for it, and so will your parents.

You are not alone if your parents don't seem to want you around. Sarah Bernhardt, a famous French actress, was rejected by her mother. She was put out into the streets because she was "in the way." Her mother wanted a clear field for all of her boyfriends. Sarah wandered around eating from garbage cans and sleeping wherever she could. One day she saw her mother in the street and begged her to let her come home. Her mother, too ashamed to say no because her latest boyfriend was with her, said okay. Sarah grew up being careful not to be a burden to her mother. Yet Sarah took that early rejection and turned it into angry energy— a determination to make people love and want her. By the time she died (in her seventies), she had millions of people weeping over her death, and her boyfriend (in his twenties) tried to jump into her grave because he didn't think he could live without her.[2] I'd say she turned the tables, wouldn't you?

Many parents are too free with their slaps and punches and use of straps and sticks and other forms of physical punishment. One young lady, Keesha, 14, says,

My English teacher noticed that my arm was swollen up twice the size of the other. She kept me after class and asked what happened. First I lied and told her I slammed it in a door. Then I started crying, and I told her how my mother beat me with a stick because I got the wrong thing from the store.

Keesha goes on to tell how her English teacher called the child abuse center and had them investigate. The story has a happy ending. The social worker from the center contacted the parent and set up an appointment for a family meeting. Keesha is now staying in a residence for

---

[2]This story appears in the book *Madam Sarah* by Cornelia Otis Skinner (Boston: Houghton Mifflin Company, 1967).

teens located about two miles from her home, and her mother is seeing a psychologist. Keesha and her mother visit each other regularly and are starting to have a good mother-daughter relationship.

If your parents are physically abusing you and no adult steps in to save you, save yourself. Call the child abuse center in your area. You can get the number from information. If you don't want to identify yourself you can pretend you are a neighbor who wishes not to be identified. Give them all the details, and they will take it from there. Don't worry. They're not going to come with a wagon and cart your parents away. They're experts in dealing with such problems, and they care about your parents, too. They're going to handle it so that in the end your parents are happy, too.

People who come from homes where they were physically abused have turned out to be very successful in spite of their early terror. Allen Wheelis is an example. Now a famous psychologist, Wheelis tells his story in his book *How People Change*. He tells how as a young teen he was supposed to mow the lawn but didn't. As a punishment his father made him stay out in the hot sun from dawn till dusk cutting the lawn with a razor blade day after day. His hands were blistered and he suffered severe burns from the sun. One day he asked his mother to help him to get out of it, and when she did, his father caught on and beat him until he could hardly move.[3] Allen's father thought that he was being a good father. He believed that he was teaching his son a lesson in being responsible. In those days there were no child abuse centers. People had to live with their abusive parents. They had to either buckle under and be destroyed or *survive*. Wheelis chose to survive. Now he is a psychologist who helps thousands of people to make better lives for themselves. He turned his early teen horror into later-life success. He used his pain to make him more compassionate toward others who suffer. You can do it, too.

[3]Allen Wheelis, *How People Change* (New York: Harper & Row, 1973).

Parents who are usually drunk or high are what I call "absentee" parents. They're not there for you because they're always off in another world. You have to be a parent not only to yourself but to them also. It certainly isn't fair. Rita, 14, says,

> My mother is usually drunk. When I come home from school, she's wasted. My father isn't much better. I never see him, and when I do, I think he's high on coke or something. I have to take care of my two younger brothers. If I didn't feed them, they'd starve to death.

Rita could try talking to her mother when she's sober. Sometimes it works. One mother says,

> I used to drink every afternoon. One day Terry said, "Mom. Please. Stop drinking. You're ruining all of our lives." I had been thinking of going to Alcoholics Anonymous. I did, and now I'm free of it. Her little speech did it.

If a talk doesn't work (and chances are it won't, because drinking can be very deep-rooted), speak to relatives and friends of the family and ask them to help to get your parent professional attention. You could also call the child abuse center. They would send someone out to help your parent to handle his or her drinking problem. You shouldn't have to go it alone. Keep searching until you find someone who will help, not just for your sake but for your parent's sake as well.

The most destructive form of parental abuse is sexual abuse. Parents who misuse their children and teenagers in such a way are desperately in need of therapy. Today it is coming out into the open that not only do fathers approach their daughters, but mothers approach their sons. Parents who do this are suffering from severe mental problems, and the best thing you can do for them and yourself is to report them.

Sandy, 14, says,

My father tried to get fresh with me and I thought I was imagining it. Then when he tried again, I almost threw up. My own father? I don't know what to do. I try to stay away from him.

Joe, 16, says,

I told my mother not to walk around without clothes in front of me. It's embarrassing. She starts trying to hug me and all that. I think it's sick.

Sandy and Joe should of course tell their abusing parent clearly that they must stop. If it happens a second time, the behavior must be reported. First tell your other parent. If nothing changes, tell another adult you trust. If that doesn't work, call child abuse. It takes a lot of courage to reveal such an ugly and sad secret, but you really have no choice. It is normal for you to be afraid to tell. As Dr. Scott M. Peck says, in his book *The Road Less Traveled*, "Courage is not the absence of fear, it is the taking of action in spite of fear."[4]

Be afraid. But then take action. You'll save yourself from being a person with deep psychological problems. If you get help now, before the problem sets in, you can be a normal, happy adult. If you hide it and let it build up inside, you will probably be mentally paralyzed for life. Save yourself. Do something now.

I've always been fascinated with the subject of the human will. I've wondered why some people, in spite of all kinds of odds against them, make it, succeed, become successful and happy, while others who seem to have everything handed to them often become losers—miserable examples of human failure. In my research, I've come across some amazing findings. The research seems to point out that a remarkably high percentage of high achievers come from backgrounds where the parents were severely

[4]Scott M. Peck, M.D., *The Road Less Traveled* (New York: Simon & Schuster, 1978), p. 131.

disturbed and where the individuals suffered all sorts of childhood and teen traumas. An educated guess as to why this is true is, such people were never allowed to take life lightly or to simply coast along. They were forced to be alert and drive hard every step of the way in order to survive. Psychologists don't know whether it is in spite of or because of these difficult early years that these people were able to reach the heights of success, they only know that there seems to be a pattern.[5]

In my own experience, those people who have a tough childhood-teen life are either destroyed by it or made stronger. The way I see it, the choice is yours. Either you're going to buckle under and let life walk all over you, or you're going to get tough and start fighting. What's it going to be? Will I be reading about you someday, the way you, in spite of all the odds, became somebody beautiful, somebody important?

Here are some reminders when dealing with problem parents.

1. Remember that anyone can have children. That's why your parents can have severe problems and still have had you.

2. Your problem parent is suffering a great deal. He or she is trying to be a good parent, but because of mental turmoil that he or she cannot control, he or she cannot be a good parent.

3. Show compassion and understanding for your parents' problem.

4. Remember that neurotic parents often project their own guilt onto you.

5. Express love and appreciation for your problem parents.

[5]Rollo May, *Freedom and Destiny* (New York: W. W. Norton & Company, 1981), p. 36. May discusses a study done by Jerome Kagan.

6. Don't accuse your parents. This will only make matters worse.

7. Parents who say they can't wait to get rid of you really mean they can't cope with the responsibility of being parents because they have too many problems of their own.

8. If your parents are physically or sexually abusing you, report them to the child abuse center in your area. You need not give your name, just the information.

9. If one of your parents is usually drunk or high, ask family or friends to help you to get your parent into a help center. If no one is available, report your parent to the child abuse center.

10. Remember that studies show that a remarkably high percentage of high achievers come from backgrounds where parents were severely disturbed and where the individuals suffered all sorts of childhood and teen traumas.

11. You have a choice: You can either buckle under or fight like a madman. What's it going to be?

Here is a chart that will help you to use some of the ideas in this chapter. Read the sample situation and then fill in the chart with your own experiences.

SAMPLE SITUATION

My mother said, "I curse the day you were born."

WRONG REACTION
"I curse the day I got stuck with you for a mother."

RESULT
We kept screaming at each other.

NEW REACTION
"I know I give you a hard time sometimes. It must be hard to be a parent."

RESULT
My mother calmed down and said, "I'm sorry, honey. I love you. I'm just feeling edgy today."

TYPICAL SITUATION

WRONG REACTION   **RESULT**

NEW REACTION   **RESULT**

TYPICAL SITUATION

WRONG REACTION   **RESULT**

NEW REACTION   **RESULT**

TYPICAL SITUATION

WRONG REACTION   **RESULT**

NEW REACTION   **RESULT**

10

Why Did She Have to Marry Him?

You didn't have enough trouble already. You really needed this. A stepparent. An intruder—an outsider to butt his or her nose into your business. Why did your real parent have to ruin everything by bringing this person into your home?

16-year-old Rob says,

> The only good thing about my stepfather is that he makes my mother happy. Otherwise he's a complete waste.

Rob shows unusual insight. Most teenagers don't stop to think of the situation from their parents' point of view because they're so busy thinking about how much they are inconvenienced by the "intruder." If your parent remarried, obviously your parent did so with the goal of being happy. You see it differently. You see this outsider as a threat to your real parent's role in your life, the one who is not living with you. You imagine this person—a cheap imitation of your real parent—trying to take over a role that he or she could never fulfill. In addition, the step's presence is a miserable reminder to you that your real parent is gone. "Oh, why can't things be the way they used to be," you may say every time you see your step.

If your real parent has died, this problem can be especially acute. On top of wishing that things could be as they once were, chances are in your mind you have glorified the past. (In fact, you may do this even if your parent is alive!) But no one could possibly measure up to a parent whose down side (there always is one) you have forgotten and whose good side remains ever-present in your mind. No stepparent can compete with a painful loss and a loving memory you hold close to your heart.

It may interest you to know, however, that your stepparent may be feeling you are difficult to have around as well. "Who needs ———. He/she is not my child. Why should I put up with all this nonsense."

Since you and your stepparent are unwilling bedfellows to say the least, it looks as if you'll have to make the best of it. After all, you can't snap your fingers and will him or her away, and your step can't make you disappear either. What you have to do is to first accept the facts. Your parent has a right to be happy. You will eventually (between three and six years probably) leave home permanently. Your parent's life will go on. He or she has to make a life that will last even after you go. This is right and normal.

Okay. You didn't ask for it. It happened to you. It looks as if fate has thrown a dagger at you. What are you going to do; let the dagger kill you? Why not interfere and make this seemingly "bad luck" event work for you. Norman Vincent Peale, world famous positive thinker and philosopher says,

> When fate throws a dagger at you . . . if you catch it
> by the handle you can use it to fight your way
> through.[1]

Fate has thrown some daggers my way. I used to work out in a popular health spa. Since I like to train with heavier weights, I would go into the men's gym area all the time. As it turned out, there was a rule, "No women in the men's gym." I protested, claiming that when I joined, I was told I could use all the facilities. I kept going into the men's gym, and the manager kept asking me to leave. Finally, I was asked to accept a refund of my membership. In short, I was being kicked out of the gym. I felt terrible. Where would I go? I was used to the routine. The gym was conveniently located. I felt disgusted and depressed.

The next day I opened the *Yellow Pages* and started calling gyms. I found one located an even shorter distance from my home, but it was a regular bodybuilding gym. No frills. To make a long story short, I joined that gym, and there I met the world-champion bodybuilders (the owner was one himself), where, in a short time and with fewer hours spent, I was able to totally transform my body into the shape that won me contest after contest and eventually evolved into my both writing for a well-known bodybuilding magazine and writing books on bodybuilding.

Instead of letting fate stab me with the dagger it threw, instead of saying, "See what I mean. Bad luck," and using it as an excuse to fail, to quit working out, I made it turn out for the best. I found a better gym at a closer distance and I trained more efficiently.

If you look carefully, there's good in every seemingly bad situation. You have to make the good emerge. If you get fired from a job, get a better job at a higher salary. If your boyfriend or girlfriend breaks up with you, meet a more desirable one, and so on. In this case, if there's a

[1] Norman Vincent Peale, *You Can If You Think You Can* (Englewood Cliffs, New Jersey: Prentice Hall), p. 307.

"stranger" in your home, make that stranger work for you instead of against you. Here's how.

Did you ever notice how much easier it is for you to talk to some of your friends' parents than it is to talk to your own? Doesn't it at times seem that every other teenager has understanding parents expect you? And did you ever wonder why some of your friends think that your parents are so great, when you are always fighting with them. The simple truth is, it's always easier to talk objectively to someone who is not "blood-related." When your real parent tries to talk to you, he or she has so much emotion invested in it that it is often impossible for him or her to be helpful to you. Not so with a nonblood parent.

You can use your stepparent as a source of information—someone to bounce ideas off—to get opinions from. You can discuss your ideas and problems with him or her without worrying that he or she will push you in a given direction because he or she has some preconceived idea on what he or she wants you to be. In effect, you can try to think of the step as an adult consultant.

The thing is, this won't work right away. There are some problems you have to get through first. So let's explore them.

I've spoken to hundreds of teenagers who have to put up with stepparents, and as a result I've concluded that the problems fall into a few major categories.

First, there is an unwillingness on the part of teenagers to talk to their steps, and there is also an unwillingness on the part of many steps to "push" too hard to get that communication. Second, teenagers resent the fact that the stepparent is different from the real parent, and there is anger on the part of the stepparent that the teenager constantly compares him or her unfavorably with the real parent. Third, teenagers resent stepparents' trying to influence or control them in any way, and steps resent the fact that they are not accepted in any role at all. They feel left out. Fourth, teenagers resent the attention the step gets from the real parent and feel as if he or she is being neglected, and the stepparent often resents the teenager's presence as being a threat to the time he or she could spend with the parent, especially if that teen is always in trouble (and takes lots of time away from the relationship he or she has with the real parent). Fifth, when the step has children of his or her own who move into the home, the teenagers resent the stepparent's favoring his or her own children, and the stepparent resents the jealousy of the teen for his or her paying attention to his or her own child.

– "I DON'T HAVE TO EXPLAIN MYSELF TO HER!" –

Poor communication, the biggest problem, can be seen as this teenager says,

> I never talk to him, and he never talks to me. I never tried to do anything nice for him, and he never did anything nice for me.

> *Dom, 15*

Dom's stepfather says,

> You can't change him, and I'm *not* going to change. It's no use talking to him.

As long as both parties stick to their guns, nothing will change. In fact things may get worse until Dom leaves home earlier than he would want to.

In order to break the negative pattern, Dom has to take the first step. What if he surprised his stepfather by asking his advice about a problem. He could talk about a situation involving a girl. Most men love to be consulted about how to handle women. They may not always give good advice, but who cares. It doesn't hurt to listen to what someone has to say, does it? Even if the advice is inappropriate, at least you would learn more about the way your stepparent's mind works. Dom's father would feel flattered that Dom consulted him. He would feel important, and he would find himself liking Dom more.

To keep the positive trend going, Dom, at the right moment, could approach his stepfather and say something like

> I've been thinking about you a lot lately; I mean the way you and I fight. It dawned on me that the same way I always say you get on my nerves, I probably get on yours. I thought it would be hard to take, but I'd like to know what it is about me, my attitude, that bothers you. Could we exchange a list of things, and then maybe we could both work on trying to make life easier for each other.

If Dom did this, his stepfather would be very surprised. It isn't every day that a teenager asks an adult to give him or her a list of things "wrong" with his or her behavior. Adults are always giving this list to teenagers, unasked, and teenagers usually throw it back in their faces with a list of excuses as to why they are always right. Dom's stepfather would most likely write up a list and then ask to see Dom's list. The two of them could make an agreement to exchange point for point. For example, Dom's list may read, "I hate when you shout at me." His stepfather's list may read, "I can't stand it when you don't answer me when I'm talking to you." Both parties could agree to change their behavior. In the above example, Dom would work on answering his stepfather, and his stepfather would try not to shout at Dom. Then, if either Dom or his stepfather forgets and begins to violate the agreement, they could remind each other about the deal.

If you begin talking to each other, you won't hate each other as much. Silence is a form of hostility. Even on an elevator, strangers will make small talk. They say things like "Some weather we're having," or "Good morning," not because they really want to discuss weather or wish each other happiness. They speak to really say, "I am not planning to do you harm. I have no evil intentions toward you." They want to make the atmosphere friendly by breaking the silence.

The longer you remain silent toward your stepparent, the more the hostility builds and the more you imagine that your step wishes you ill. Your step also imagines all sorts of things about you. "He hates me," your step thinks. "She can't stand me," your step imagines. Be a "mench" (real person) and break the ice. Make something happen.

Another way to break the ice is to do something kind for your stepparent. A 39-year-old stepmother says,

> I'll never forget it. My stepdaughter gave me a gift for mother's day. I was shocked because I know she doesn't think of me as her mother. Later, I overheard her telling her friend that she got me a gift because she didn't want me to feel left out. It really made me feel good that she was concerned with my feelings.

You don't have to buy your step a mother's or father's day gift. You can buy a surprise gift, something cute, something you think he or she would appreciate. It could be something related to a sport he or she engages in or a hobby he has. If you do this, your step will automatically like you more because he or she will sense that you like him or her. When someone thinks you like him or her, that person starts liking you. I once did an experiment to prove this. I used to attend a church where there were two young men who seemed to despise one another. Whenever I was around one, he would say something negative about the other, and vice versa. One day I told the first young man, You know that brother (we used to call each other "sister" and "brother" in the church) ———— he really admires you. He told me he was watching your style and he . . . His face lit up and he said, "Really?" quite surprised. At the next opportunity I spoke to the second young man and said, You know that brother ———— was talking about you and he said he really admires you. The man's face lit up and he said, "No kidding." The next week I couldn't help laughing when I saw the two of them at the back of the church having a lively conversation, laughing and talking together. Neither of these two young men had any use for the other until I made them believe that the one admired the other!

Do you see what I'm driving at? You have to let your step see that you like him or her—That you have use for, that you in some way admire him or her. You might even start a conversation with your step about his or her job. You could ask questions about how hard the job is and how people must look up to him or her. There are many ways to express acceptance toward your stepparent. If you make the first move, your effort will be rewarded by your step accepting you and making your life less miserable.

Finally, you could give your stepparent an honest compliment once in a while. Why not say something like "You look great in that shirt," or "How do you keep in such good shape?" Everyone loves a compliment. Watch the way your step warms up to you if you start complimenting him or her. You'll probably get a few compliments back right away. If you study your step, I'm sure you can find something good to say.

– "MY REAL FATHER IS SMARTER THAN YOU!" –

Probably one of the biggest things you hold against your step is the fact that he or she is not as good as your real mother or father. Because you automatically make this comparison in your mind, your step hasn't got a chance to come up favorably. But who says your step has to be anything like your real parent. In fact the more unlike your real parent your step is, the better off you are. Your real parent is your ideal. No one can or should ever take his or her place. Now that you've got that out of the way, perhaps you can forgive your step for not measuring up. Maybe you won't say things like Ronny, 15:

> If I could create a perfect stepfather he would be just like my real father.

Stepparents hate to be compared to your real parents. They know they are fighting a losing battle. A 41-year-old stepfather says,

> All I ever hear is, "My father this and my father gives me that, and my father never..." In the meantime the guy's a real jerk—always drunk, but he'd never admit that.

You see. Comparing only makes this stepfather become defensive. He finds ways to say that the real parent is in fact inferior to him, whether or not it is true. This is human nature. Whenever people are attacked, they defend themselves. Don't you do the same thing when someone tries to compare you unfavorably to someone else?

Instead of comparing your stepparent to your real parent, how about making a conscious effort to separate the two in your own mind. Put your real parent in the special high position you hold for him or her—far above your stepparent. Then look at your step and study him or her for positive qualities. Make a list of all the things you like about him or her. I'm sure you just said in your mind, "Nothing." But if you think hard, you'll come up with a few things. You may find that he or she is intelligent, has a good sense of humor, dresses well, earns a good salary, is generous, shows an interest in you, offers to drive you places, invites you to join him or her in a sport or hobby. Once you have the list, every time you start thinking about all the negative qualities regarding your stepparent, think of his or her good points. Learn to accent the positive. If you do this, you may find yourself forgiving your stepparent for not being better than he or she is, and if you remember to stop comparing him or her to your real parent, you may even forgive your step for not being as good or being different from your real parent. In fact you'll be glad that he or she is not as good. After all, you already have your real parent. Just because that parent isn't living with you anymore doesn't mean he or she isn't your parent any more.

– "YOU CAN'T TELL ME WHAT TO DO, YOU'RE NOT MY PARENT!" –

The third problem teenagers have with stepparents— not wanting to let that step have any say about anything, can be seen in the following comments.

He thinks he can tell me what to do. Why doesn't he mind his own business.

Bobby, 16

I just don't want her around. Who needs her butting her nose into my business, asking questions. I don't even want to talk to her.

Tracy, 15

(Living with her father and stepmother)

My mother lets my stepfather influence her mind.
I hate him for that.

Tony, 17

What these teenagers don't realize is that the stepparents don't really want to boss them around or try to take the place of the real parent. All they want is to be accepted as something in the lives of the teenagers. They want to have a place.

This 45 year old stepfather says,

I don't want to be his father. I have kids of my own. I just want to have some influence on his life—help in some way.

A 36-year-old stepmother says,

All I want is for my stepdaughter to accept me as a person. I don't want to be her mother. Just a big sister, no—not that—more of a guide to her.

A 39-year-old stepfather says,

He doesn't think I'm his parent or even his guardian. He doesn't think I'm anything to him.

A 37-year-old stepmother says,

I know things from experience. Why can't she listen to my ideas.

A 41-year-old stepfather says,

Hey, I don't want to play the role of policeman or father or not even boss. I just want to give him some direction.

They're giving themselves away. They're telling you exactly what it would take to make them happy and get them off your back. Don't you see. All you have to do is let them talk to you, let them give you their opinions and ideas. Let them try to influence you. All of your teachers try to influence you, don't they? Of course they don't all succeed, right? What harm would it be to listen to your stepparent, to act interested when he or she talks to you?

No one is forcing you to follow their ideas. If you think about it, you are influenced by hundreds of things in a given week. Television, newspapers, books, friends, teachers, parents, relatives, things you see, memories— all of these have an influence on your behavior and on your decisions. Yet it is *you* who, after putting everything together, comes up with the final decision as to what you will or will not do. You are in no danger of turning into a robot and automatically following the commands of your stepparents, so stop being so afraid to listen to what they have to say. Once you do, you'll find that they relax and get off your case. Your life will be more pleasant.

Instead of hoping his stepfather minds his own business, what would happen if Bobby asked for his opinion now and then? Instead of not talking to her stepmother, what if Tracy not only answered her stepmother's questions but asked her questions about her own life and interests? Instead of hating his stepfather for influencing his mother's mind, what if Tony asked him to help him with his homework? The step parents would be flattered. They would feel needed. They would feel important. And yes. They would lighten up.

– "EVER SINCE YOU CAME, NO ONE PAYS ANY ATTENTION TO ME!" –

Teenagers resent the fact that the stepparent takes the time and attention of the real parent away from them, and stepparents often resent the teenager's taking the time of the real parent away from them.

My mother used to go shopping with me all the time. Now she's always too busy. . . .

Stephanie, 14

My mother is always out with him. The two of them are always together. It's sickening.

Eric, 15

Stepparents complain

That boy is always demanding attention. She's letting him rule her life. I think he does it on purpose to interfere with us.

Diane plays up to her father. She knows just how to get his attention, and he falls for it every time.

Jealousy. It's clear that both teens and steps are protective of the attention of the real parent. Jealousy is nothing to be ashamed of. It's caused by something most of us live with—insecurity. We are afraid of losing something we need—in this case the time and attention of the real parent. But if you think about it objectively, your chances of losing the love, time, and attention of your real parent are very slim. As a matter of fact you should probably be glad that your real parent has someone to divert his or her attention away from you. You really don't need twenty-four-hour attention from your real parent. Lots of teenagers who live with single parents complain that the parents are always "on their backs" because they have nothing better to do with their time. Actually it's healthy for your real parent to have a social and romantic life, so be glad your step is there to supply it.

As far as your step's being jealous of you, he or she will have to come to the realization that you need not pose a threat despite the negative environment you help to create. If you can't stand your stepparent, then you probably wish your step would be put out of the house. Chances are your step feels and fears your anger, is jealous of the time your parent spends with you, and worries that you will eventually have your way and cause him or her to be thrown out. Of course adults are not supposed to be insecure. They're "supposed" to be in control—

calm, dignified, above it all. But the truth is, adults are only teenagers in aging skin. They usually feel most of the same insecurities, only different forms of them, that teenagers feel. They, too, need to see that the threat they feel can disappear.

What can you do to make the situation better? Instead of putting your real parent on the spot, making him or her feel as if he or she is being torn between you and your stepparent, why not take a mature stance. Realize that your real parent has his or her show to run and you have yours. Look at your step as your real parent's social life, and let him or her have it. You wouldn't want your social life taken away. You may think, "Social life. Ha. That boring ———" Yes. To your parent that step is the equivalent of your social life, and to you, your social life is important, and as exciting as you make it. Live and let live. Give your parents a break. Once you let up on your resentment and anger, you stepparent will stop being fearful and jealous of you. You might even have a talk with him or her one day when you are in a good mood. You might tell your step that you were doing a lot of thinking and that you realize how silly it was for you to resent him or her. Tell your step that you are glad that your real parent is happy and that you are happy because of that fact. Tell him or her that you want to make his or her life easier and that you will try to be more cooperative.

If do do this, your stepparent will be relieved and will stop looking at you as an enemy who is trying to get rid of him or her.

– "YOU ONLY LISTEN TO YOUR OWN KID!" –

If your stepparent has children, you may feel that he or she is paying special attention to those children at your expense. Tammy, 14, says,

I'm the one who gets stuck doing all the housework. Her children just lounge around and get away with murder.

Livia, 17, says,

My stepmother is always insinuating that her bratty kids are smarter than I am. She'll say things like "You know, Livia, there's no reason you can't get As just like Karen and Peter do." I usually get Bs. She's always helping them with their homework. I think she does it for them.

Tammy and Livia may be right. It would be the most natural thing in the world for a person to favor his or her real children over stepchildren. Don't you favor your real parent over your stepparent? But don't despair. Your stepparents don't believe it's right for them to show favoritism, and they try really hard not to. One stepfather says,

When my own son came to live with us, I made up my mind not to treat him special. Yet I find myself doing little things for him that I wouldn't do for her children. When the other kids complain, I usually make up a lot of excuses, but I know I'm wrong.

A stepmother says,

How stupid. Of course you're going to favor your own children. You can't help it. They're your own flesh and blood. Any stepchild should understand that. As long as you don't overdo it.

Another stepmother says,

I have two of my own children and one of his. His girl is thirteen, and she has more responsibilities around the house than my two because mine are younger, nine and eleven. She's always saying I'm not fair, but I know I am. Someday she'll understand.

Compromise is the key to peaceful existence in the case where your step has children living in your home. Realize that blood ties are stronger than formed bonds. Allow your stepparent to favor his or her own children just a little, but if it gets out of hand, protest. You might say something like

I know that ———— is your real child and it's normal for you to give him special attention. But sometimes I feel like the stepchild in the fairy tales. It doesn't seem fair that I get to do more work and that you never say nice things to me. It may be my fault, because I probably give you a hard time most of the time....

Such a speech would alert the step to the fact that you are aware of favoring, and it would also take him or her off the defensive (the fact that you said it may be your fault). Your step would probably be more alert to his or her attitudes and might change and treat you more fairly.

Your job is to help your stepparent not to feel guilty for favoring his or her own children. If you accuse your step and say something like

Don't think I don't see how your own children get away with everything....

Your step will merely defend him or herself. You might even say that you would favor your own kids if you were a stepparent, even though you don't think it's right. Once your step doesn't feel as if he or she were on trial, your step will lower his or her defense and you can make progress.

Here are some reminders to help you when dealing with stepparents.

1. Your stepparent is threatened by your presence just the same way you are threatened by his or her presence.

2. You cannot make your stepparent disappear, so you might as well turn a seemingly bad situation into a good one by using your stepparent as an adult friend.

3. Break the communication barrier with your stepparent by asking for advice, asking to exchange lists of things that bother you both about each other, giving honest compliments, giving thoughtful gifts, etc.

4. Stop mentally comparing your stepparent with your real parent. Realize that one has nothing to do with the other.

5. Compile a list of positive qualities possessed by your stepparent.

6. Help your stepparent to feel less threatened by you by letting him or her have some of your real parent's time. Learn to live and let live. Your parent needs a social life.

7. Remember that your stepparent can never steal your real parent away from you. You will always have a sacred place in your parent's life.

8. If you think that your stepparent is favoring his or her own children over you, help them to feel less guilty about it by showing them that you consider it normal. You will see that the unfair treatment lessens.

Here is a chart that will help you to use some of the information gained in this chapter. Read the sample situation and then fill in the chart with your own experiences.

SAMPLE SITUATION

My stepfather said, "Are you sure you have enough money?" (I was on my way out the door to meet a girl for a date.)

WRONG REACTION
"No. I'm an idiot. I only
have a dollar."

RESULT
"Don't be so sarcastic. I was
just trying to help, but you're
always so nasty, so what's
the use?"

NEW REACTION
"I have thirty dollars. That
should be enough, don't you
think?"

RESULT
Offered me another twenty
dollars, "just in case." I left
the house in a good mood,
and he was smiling.

TYPICAL SITUATION

WRONG REACTION

RESULT

NEW REACTION

RESULT

TYPICAL SITUATION

WRONG REACTION

RESULT

NEW REACTION

RESULT

TYPICAL SITUATION

WRONG REACTION   **RESULT**

NEW REACTION   **RESULT**

A Final Note—
Why Bother

Lets face it. The cavalry isn't coming over the hill to save you. Nobody is going to suddenly appear and magically change your life. The people you were counting on are never there when you need them. They're always out to lunch.

You will have to be your own rescue team. Instead of looking for the genie with the lamp that can be rubbed and give you any wish you desire, look at the genius in your own brain. Look for the cavalry in the courage of your own heart.

I once read the following words, and I leave them with you as a final message:

The haves and the have nots can be traced back to the dids and did nots.[1]

It's up to you. Are you going to do something or are you going to wait around and hope to get lucky?

[1] M. R. Kopmeyer, *How to Get Whatever You Want* (Louisville, Kentucky: M. R. Kopmeyer, 1972), p. 36.

– BIBLIOGRAPHY –

Horney, Karen., M.D. *Neurosis and Human Growth*. New York: W. W. Norton & Company, 1950.

Jung, Carl G. *Memories, Dreams, Reflections*. Edited by Amelia Jaffe. Translated by Richard and Clara Winston. New York: Random House, Vintage Books, 1961.

Kiev, Ari, M.D. *Riding Through the Downers, Hassles, Snags and Funks*. New York: E. P. Dutton & Company, 1980.

Kopmeyer, M.R. *How to Get Whatever You Want*. Louisville, Kentucky: M. Kopmeyer, 1972.

Maslow, Abraham. *Toward a Psychology of Being*. New York: D. Van Nostrand Company, 1968.

May, Rollo. *The Courage to Create*. New York: Bantam Books, 1975.

May, Rollo. *Freedom and Destiny*. New York: W. W. Norton & Company, 1981.

May, Rollo. *Love and Will*. New York: Dell Publishing Company, 1969.

Offer, Daniel, M.D. "Adolescent Turmoil." *Landmarks in Literature*. *New York University Quarterly* (Winter, 1982).

Peale, Norman Vincent. *You Can If You Think You Can*. Englewood Cliffs, New Jersey: Prentice Hall, 1975.

Peck, Scott, M.D. *The Road Less Traveled*. New York: Simon & Schuster, 1978.

Sherman, Harold. *The New TNT*. Englewood Cliffs, New Jersey: Prentice Hall, 1966.

Skinner, Cornelia Otis. *Madam Sarah*. Boston: Houghton Mifflin Company, 1967.

Wheelis, Allen. *How People Change*. New York: Harper & Row, 1973.

Vedral, Joyce, Ph.D. *I Dare You*. New York: Ballantine Books, 1983.

Joyce Vedral, a Ph.D. in English Literature, teaches English at Julia Richman High School in New York City. She is also an adjunct professor in English at Pace University.

She has written for *Seventeen Magazine* and *Parents Magazine*, and is a regular contributor to *Muscle and Fitness Magazine*.

Joyce is the author of I DARE YOU, I CAN'T TAKE IT ANY MORE, and THE OPPOSITE SEX IS DRIVING ME CRAZY, self-help books for teens. She has also written NOW OR NEVER, PERFECT PARTS, HARD BODIES, THE HARD BODIES EXPRESS WORKOUT, and SUPERCUT, all books dealing with physical fitness.

After touring the United States, Joyce has discovered by interviewing countless teenagers, that their number one concern is: How to get along with parents. For this reason, she decided to devote an entire book to that subject.

Joyce is involved in many sports, among them bodybuilding, Jiu-Jitsu, Karate, and Judo. She has won bodybuilding contests and holds a series of belts in each of the three branches of the martial arts.

Marthe Vedral is an eleventh grade student who is a valuable source of inside information on the way teenagers really feel. She often helps her mother with decisions concerning the appropriateness of her material. She is a green belt in Tae Kwon Do Karate, and is involved in bodybuilding. She is planning to become a psychologist.